# THE INSIDER'S SECRETS TO GETTING YOUR SCHOOL LEADERSHIP JOB

# THE INSIDER'S SECRETS TO GETTING YOUR SCHOOL LEADERSHIP JOB

DR. LARRY ARONSTEIN

 FIRST HILL BOOKS

FIRST HILL BOOKS
An imprint of Wimbledon Publishing Company
*www.anthempress.com*

This edition first published in UK and USA 2023
by FIRST HILL BOOKS
75–76 Blackfriars Road, London SE1 8HA, UK
or PO Box 9779, London SW19 7ZG, UK
and
244 Madison Ave #116, New York, NY 10016, USA

*British Library Cataloguing-in-Publication Data*
A catalogue record for this book is available from the British Library.

*Library of Congress Control Number: 2023901505*
A catalog record for this book has been requested.

ISBN-13: 978-1-83998-895-0 (Pbk)
ISBN-10: 1-83998-895-9 (Pbk)

This title is also available as an e-book.

# CONTENTS

# Contents

# INTRODUCTION

For 50 years, I have served as a school leader, as a superintendent of schools, an assistant superintendent for curriculum and instruction, a school principal at all levels, and the director of the Long Island Leadership Academy. I have had the privilege of teaching, supervising, nurturing, and mentoring hundreds of aspiring, newly appointed, and veteran school leaders. I believe my 50 years of experiences have provided me with a deep and practical understanding of school leadership. I have interviewed and hired more than a thousand leaders over the years. Nevertheless, I make no excuses for the imperfect, flawed, and sometimes nepotistic personnel practices that are too often in play across many educational systems. As a native New Yorker, I sometimes sum up our powerlessness to change a system that is rooted in school systems by saying, "It is what it is!" You've just got to work with what you have.

I'm sorry to say that as a young educator who was just starting my career as a school leader, I had few mentors and no roadmap. What I was able to learn was based on trial and error—mostly errors. The result was confusion, frustration, and even anger that my job applications led to few interviews and those interviews were unsuccessful. My confusion grew out of my ignorance about how the application process really worked. The frustration was my personal reaction to trying my best and feeling that less talented people were getting the jobs. My anger was fueled by being the runner-up and never the chosen one. Even as I grew to better understand the "game," I still had not mastered the nuances. I promised myself, many years ago, that when I was in an influential leadership role, I would mentor talented, aspiring leaders so they would not have to suffer as I had.

This book is my attempt to keep my promise by guiding the reader to successfully cope with the existing system of recruiting and hiring school leaders. I dig into the fabric of how the process really works from the inside. What I offer you are my unique, tried-and-tested, and sometimes unorthodox strategies that

1

I've taught my clients over the last 12 years. I can report that, with a good deal of confidence that my strategies work. I urge you to read this book, master the strategies, and put them into practice. I predict that your journey will end with the words, "YOU'RE HIRED!"

LWA

CHAPTER 1

# KNOW WHO YOU ARE

## Investing in Yourself

Recently, a suburban school district posted an ad for an assistant principal. The district attracted more than two hundred applicants, met virtually with 25 for a prescreening interview, and then had a hiring committee of seven teachers, supervisors, and parents interview 15 semifinalists. At about the same time, the Kentucky Derby had 19 horses "Run for the Roses." Those horses had the benefit of the best trainers in the world to prepare them. Trying to get a leadership job is very much like a horse race.

How much of an investment does a serious candidate make in getting certified as a school leader? Graduate programs require application fees, tuition, books, time, and expenses for commuting. Then there is buying an interview suit or outfit. That can easily add up to more than $10,000. Does investing a small fraction of that for a coach make sense to you? What can a coach do for you? Does coaching work?

Being a well-coached competitive candidate is the difference between playing a good game of checkers and being a fine chess player. A good coach will prepare you. A coach can help you hone your resume and cover letter; present yourself with self-confidence; tell a compelling story about why you are the right match for the job; anticipate and prepare impressive and unique responses to interviewers' questions; and strategize what to say, what not to say, and how to read body language. Yes, coaching does work. Those who receive coaching do so confidentially. You do not have to let anyone know "the secret of your success."

Many universities, agencies, and consultants can provide services for preparing your resume and cover letter and providing interview tips. However, the right coach has a diverse and well-positioned network of former clients and colleagues. He or she knows the school districts and the inside information.

3

You will be guided on how to fashion your approach to the special needs and wants of the district. People who play horses get lots of tips—some good, some sketchy. We all get tips on how to invest, what restaurants to dine at, and what places to shop. A tip, of course, is just an opinion. Most of us have never made money on stock tips and can be disappointed with tips in general. But a good coach goes far beyond informal "tips." A good coach teaches you actionable, inside strategies based on thoughtful guiding principles.

A good coach gives you feedback on your interviews and assists you in closing the deal and negotiating your contract. Like any good service, you should not expect this to come free of charge. Getting promoted is a lifetime gain that requires a short-term investment. But remember: the best investment you can ever make is in yourself. All of these "investments" increase your chances of winning that leadership position. In some respects, it is a game of probability. All things being equal, the best prepared candidate has the best chance.

If you are serious about your future as a school leader, then these are the investments that you need to make. If you are not getting interviews, consider seeking feedback on your resume and cover letter from supervisors who have sat on the receiving side of thousands of credentials and know what they are reading. The purpose of your resume and cover letter is to get you an interview. If you happen to be getting interviews but are not moving along to the next step in the process and still are serious about getting that job, then perhaps you should consider engaging the services of a coach.

A coach should have the experience of being a decision-maker in interviewing and hiring school leaders. You should feel comfortable in relating to this coach and sharing your self-perceived insecurities. A good coach will help you craft your message, teach you strategies, help build your self-confidence, give you model responses, keep your reactions objective rather than subjective, role-play both sides of the table with you, and offer candid and constructive feedback. Coaching is, pure and simple, another critical investment you can make in yourself.

### Get the Job: Stand Out from Other Applicants

If you find that you have rewritten your resume and cover letter multiple times and applied for every supervisory job for which you're qualified within 40 miles but still no interviews, then what's wrong? You ask yourself, "Do only internal candidates get interviews? Is nepotism at work? Is it *me*?" As a candidate, your goal is to stand out from the rest of the field and be seen as the most qualified and desirable. You should present yourself as a solid professional with valuable knowledge and experience to offer in your new role as a leader. How do you distinguish yourself?

When you apply for a supervisory job such as an assistant principal, principal, or a department chairperson, you need to demonstrate combinations of the following four criteria: (1) significant professional accomplishments, (2) unique or well-developed skill sets and/or knowledge base in line with the qualifications for the position, (3) evidence of leadership potential, and (4) evidence of high motivation and agility.

## *1. Significant Professional Accomplishments*

Be on the lookout for unique and interesting and growthful opportunities for self-development. Examples of such opportunities might be piloting a new curriculum, field-testing new technologies, participating in a research study, publishing a manuscript in a recognized professional periodical, participating in a summer internship or national institute, presenting a paper at a regional or state conference, being recognized and/or honored by a professional educational organization, writing a report, or helping to develop and write a plan to improve an important school-wide initiative, for instance a safety plan or plan to improve student achievement.

## *2. Unique or Well-Developed Skills and Knowledge*

The goal is not to add bullets to your resume. The goal is to acquire valuable skills and knowledge and present them in the best light on your resume and during your interview. For example, your prospective principal could always use help in scheduling—master schedule, testing schedules, schedules of professional development activities, and schedules of school–community events. So, take workshops to learn how to use proven technologies and practices in scheduling.

Another key function is student discipline. Learning how experienced professionals handle student discipline is an invaluable skill set. Volunteer to shadow an administrator. Find an administrator who will allow you to be an unofficial "dean," and who will supervise you, assign you to routine disciplinary cases, and permit you to assist in supervising lunchrooms and bus duties.

## *3. Leadership*

Consider filling some quasi-administrative roles. Serving as an administrator in summer school, night school, or alternative school can help you learn key supervisory skills and be noticed by your school leaders. Another way to stand out as a leader is by serving on committees. To a considerable degree, leadership depends upon the role you play and the impact you have on committees. Volunteer to serve as a committee chairperson, write portions of plans and reports, and present at school board meetings and faculty meetings.

### 4. Motivation and Agility

Being an inside candidate is usually the best path to becoming a school leader. Do what you can within your school and district to be visible, cooperative, and useful. Voluntarily moving to another grade level and/or school demonstrates your flexibility and cooperation and increases your scope of experience. You will also be seen as a team player. Another avenue for demonstrating your motivation is to take charge of school and community events such as assembly programs, field trips, community service projects, PTA programs, and in-service programs. Finally, do not be a spectator who stands on the sidelines and expects to be noticed. Be an active presence, make yourself useful, learn all you can, and enhance your skills and knowledge. Get into the game!

### Your Candidacy: A Reality Check

You must be realistic about your qualifications and experience. Once you take stock of your strengths and deficits, you will be better able to strategize and navigate the process of getting a leadership job. You should consider your experience; the reputation of the districts you've worked in and studied in (even though those reputations may be inaccurate); your ability to be noticed and mentored by school leaders; your skills, knowledge, and accomplishments; your willingness and ability to relocate; your status as to being laid off, resigning, or denied tenure; your aspirations about working in the suburbs and leaving a city; and your commitment to enhance your qualifications by furthering your education and professional accomplishments.

### The Inexperienced Candidate

If you are *not*: (1) an inside candidate, (2) a resident in the district, (3) the holder of a degree from a prestigious university, (4) an active and visible member of a professional association, (5) the possessor of a unique skill set like school scheduling, or (6) already holding a similar position, then your chances for getting that job becomes more daunting. Still, you should consider applying for a job in what might be considered a dysfunctional district in which the pool of candidates may be limited. I understand that while "dysfunctional" is a tough word, some districts historically are political hotbeds and/or have difficult working conditions. A word of caution—be careful what you wish for! There are often good reasons behind a district having a poor reputation—it was probably earned. Many good people have tried to turn these districts around, and many, despite their best efforts, have failed. In addition, it is difficult to get a good job after working in a dysfunctional district. Unfortunately, a certain snobbery among some misguided educators suggests that you might not be a good educator because you are working in a dysfunctional place. Of course, there are many outstanding urban and urban/suburban educators. Unfortunately, I am only being brutally frank!

### Are You Willing to Relocate?

Are you frustrated that, despite doing "all the right stuff"—paying out thousands of dollars in tuition to get your administrative certificates, regularly checking job postings, sending out an endless stream of resumes, going on dead-end interviews—you feel you are going nowhere? As an alternative, have you seriously considered relocating in order to jumpstart your administrative career?

Relocating, for most people, involves a good deal of sacrifice. Moving one's family often means disrupting your spouse's career, changing your children's schools, separating from family and friends, and disconnecting from your roots. Having to travel to a job that is more than a few commuting hours away can involve finding local housing for yourself, traveling back home only on weekends, and experiencing lonely nights. However, if you are not in a committed relationship or if your partner and family are willing to move, then relocating may not be so onerous. It is an important personal and professional decision that only you and your loved ones can make.

Include several factors in your consideration.

1. Can you afford a second residence and the costs of commuting? You should expect that salaries outside affluent suburbs will be significantly lower. Of course, if you decide to live in a less affluent community, the reduced cost of living will be proportional to your salary.
2. Can you and your family adapt to the new community's values, pace of life, and lifestyle? Needless to say, those used to living in a metropolitan area may find it particularly challenging to fit in and be accepted in a new, more suburban, or rural community.

3. If you work outside of your present state of residence, what are the implications regarding your pension, health insurance, and other contractual considerations? If you leave your state permanently, think about your status in a retirement system. Are you vested in a state pension system and/ or can you buy back years in your new pension system? You may not be planning to leave your state permanently, but it can happen.

Does relocating really pay off if your plan is to get administrative experience, be a more attractive candidate, and move back? There are no guarantees. You should probably be prepared to remain in your new position until you earn tenure. Chances are you will be a more attractive candidate if you make a parallel move. Relocating to become an assistant principal, in my opinion, will not guarantee a principal position if you move back.

Finally, you need to examine your commitment to becoming a leader. There are inevitable sacrifices. However, be open to the possibility that you may settle in, love your new job, find happiness in your new community and lifestyle, and spend your career there. Your career life is a journey. Consider all the possibilities. It worked out quite well for Dr. Robert Wallis.

### Dr. Robert Wallis—On Relocation

*I was a high school social studies teacher. My classroom was located in the corner of the third-floor corridor. Supervisors seldom traveled to that part of the building. I named my corridor "Walliland" because I reigned in my own little kingdom. I'm a large man with a personality and a sense of humor which are proportional to my size. Beneath this exterior resides a very bright and creative professional, who enjoyed widespread popularity among the students who I taught and the athletes who I coached. I had completed my administrative certification program and was working on my doctorate.*

*I applied for a position as an assistant principal in a neighboring district and got the first leadership job for which I had ever applied. I believe that the forcefulness of my personality and a kind of working-class charm led to my success. With my dissertation just about completed and with three years of successful service as an assistant principal, I was offered a position in yet another school district as their high school principal. Although I never introduced myself as Dr. Wallis, everyone throughout the district and my school referred to me as Dr. Wallis. I was introduced to the community through their newsletter as Dr. Wallis. My stationery identified me as Dr. Wallis. Knowing that officially my degree would be conferred within the next few months, once the last chapter of the dissertation was completed and approved, I neglected correcting the fact that I actually shouldn't be called doctor. In mid-December, I had clearly established myself as a successful, well-liked, and effective high school principal. Late one afternoon, the superintendent requested that I come by for a chat. The superintendent, during this face-to-face meeting, confronted me about the status of the doctorate. I explained that the degree would be finalized officially in January. The superintendent inquired why I hadn't corrected the false title of Dr. Wallis. I explained that I never asked anyone to refer to me as Dr. Wallis and that my resume and job application indicated that the doctorate was pending the completion of the dissertation. The superintendent concluded that this was a serious problem. He told me that the chairman of the administration program at the university was an old friend of the superintendent, and that word had reached the chairman that I had fraudulently claimed possession of a doctorate from his university. The chairman indicated that he was going to charge me for fraudulent actions and have me removed from the university.*

*The superintendent, realizing the seriousness of this charge and the potential embarrassing public relations disaster for the school district, demanded that I resign immediately. He assured me that the reason for the resignation would be kept confidential. Shattered, confused, embarrassed, and stunned, I wrote a two-sentence letter of resignation. There I was without a job, without my doctorate, and in the middle of the school year. I told myself and my family that I'd have a new job within a few weeks. I'd even be willing to take a position as an assistant principal. I understood that I'd probably receive a cut in pay and began applying for assistant principal positions within a 40-mile radius. I was regularly contacted for interviews. In each instance, the second or third question asked of me was why I had only served from July to December as a principal. How could I answer this question honestly without looking like a fraud? Well-meaning friends suggested that I create a "plausible" story. Tell them that your wife was seriously ill and that you had to stay home to provide childcare and provide homecare to your sick wife. Tell them that you were in a serious accident and required extensive physical therapy.*

*This was all distasteful; for me, lying was out of the question. What were my references saying about me? Had rumors spread throughout the region about the circumstances of the resignation? I'd never really know the answers to those questions. The rest of the school year went by and I was still out of work. The new school year began and still no job offers. Was my career in public education ended?*

*Finally, the interviews stopped. I was now convinced that I wasn't going to get a job in public education. My wife and I decided that we'd have to relocate in order to rekindle my career. It would be difficult for Mrs. Wallis to get a new job and to uproot our young school age children from their school, neighborhood, friends, and family. But we made the painful decision to relocate.*

*Job interviews immediately began to roll in and within several weeks, I had three job offers to serve as a high school principal. I told the truth about resigning, and no one seemed to care. They understood. We sold our house and I started my new job in another state. I was able to purchase a much larger home for half as much as he had sold my old home.*

Dr. Wallis quickly attained a new job, and the children adjusted easily into their new community and school.

### Enhancing Your Qualifications

Applicants often say, "I think that I'm well qualified, but I'm just not getting interviews. How can I improve upon my resume and enhance my chances of getting interviews?" My advice starts with analyzing the job posting and then emphasizing your experience, skills, and knowledge that match the require-ments. While this may sound obvious, a surprising number of candidates are so proud of their other accomplishments in staff development and curriculum projects that they neglect the more mundane but equally vital requirements being sought. For example, most postings for assistant principal positions will mention student discipline, school management (bus and cafeteria duties), scheduling, and organizing testing programs. Principals need help, and the posted job requirements clarify the areas in which that help is needed. You must address these requirements and they should appear prominently at the top of your resume's bulleted lists and in your cover letter.

If you do not have the necessary experiences and skills, then determine what you need to do to gain them. Consider volunteering in your present posi-tion to assist with administrative assignments. Register for conferences and workshops where you can learn more about scheduling, conflict resolution, de-escalation, writing teacher evaluations, and dealing with difficult people. Join a professional group. Volunteer for a committee and/or leadership role. In short, step out of the chorus line and become a noticed presence. There is a quantum-leap difference between being visible (a member) and becoming a presence (an active participant).

Finally, make contacts and network with school leaders. Ask your supervi-sor to mentor you and to provide feedback and opportunities for your growth. Connect and follow up with your college instructors and workshop leaders. Ask for their advice. School leaders are people, too. They appreciate the respect and recognition that come with someone asking for their help. Notice how Bryan Woodson strategically gained quality experiences as they become available.

### Bryan Woodson—Gaining Quality Experiences

*I've been teaching high school English for 10 years. Colleagues say that the initial impression that I make is that of being an intelligent, reserved, kind, thoughtful, and capable profes-sional. I teach several AP (advanced placement) courses. These courses usually assigned to the most highly experienced and respected members of our department. I've twice been selected by the students of the senior class to speak at their graduation ceremonies. This honor goes to the most respected and popular teachers. I also serve as the secretary of our teachers' union. Being an officer in the union is an indication of trust and respect from one's colleagues. I've also served on key curriculum and staff development committees and am quite knowledgeable about the most important new trends in public education.*

*My resume appears strong enough to get me more than my share of interviews. As a result of working on my interviewing skills, I've consistently moved forward to next steps in the interviewing processes. However, I've not been able to land the job. Logic tells me that if you come close to getting the job several times, then sooner or later you'll succeed. Yet, I thought that strategy could take several years. What can I now do to enhance my chances? I need leadership and supervisory experience.*

*I noticed personnel posting in my district for principal of the Evening High School and am now serving in this position. The job description calls for the recruiting, supervising, and evaluating of teachers; scheduling; student management—all functions that go into running a school, except scaled down in size. Although some might refer to running a night school, a summer school, or an alternative school as quasi-administrative experiences, these experiences are real. There are a lot of authentic leadership skills to be learned. I am enhancing my resume and can only be a stronger candidate as a result of taking on this assignment. Perhaps even more importantly, now that I'm actually functioning as a leader and supervising a staff, I am getting a reality check. I'm finding that I'm actually a strong and decisive leader. I really enjoy the role.*

*It might take years of continuing to just interview over and over again before I might finally land a job. Interviewing does not enhance my resume and my skills. I believe that taking on "quasi-leadership" jobs will accelerate my progress. It has enhanced my skills and made my resume even stronger.*

### From the City to the Suburbs

**Question**: *"I work in New York City, and I'm interested in working in the suburbs. I commute one hour each way. I am not getting interviews when I apply to suburban schools nearer to my home. What can I do?"*

There is a barrier, an often-unspoken barrier. Part-mythology, part-snobbery, it has been long thought that urban educators' experiences cannot transfer their experiences and skills to the suburbs because of the cultural. However, this barrier can be overcome in several ways.

1. Apply to urban–suburban districts where, by definition, there is much diversity and poverty. Your urban experiences are valuable in these

schools. After earning tenure, you can then parlay working in urban–suburban schools into working in suburban schools. Although it is a longer road, you will get there.

2. Obtain your urban experience in a reputable, successful, and innovative school where you will gain state-of-the-art knowledge and a unique and desirable skill set. Urban schools often provide outstanding professional development opportunities. Take advantage of those opportunities. Make your knowledge and skills the centerpiece of your resume. Start your resume off with a category called UNIQUE KNOWLEDGE AND SKILLS, and craft bullet statements that go straight to the heart of what you know and what you can do. Emphasize these experiences near the top of your cover letter as well.

3. Volunteer to participate in leadership roles and/or special training in your present assignment. This will demonstrate your initiative. These experiences should also go to the top of your bullet list in relation to your assignment. For entry-level leadership positions (dean, assistant principal), be aware that candidates who have experience with student discipline, the use of technology, data analysis, scheduling, and classroom observations are all particularly valuable.

4. Maintain contact with colleagues who have moved to leadership positions in the suburbs. They can ask decision-makers to flag your application. You cannot overestimate the value of a good network. However, although your contacts might be able to have someone review your qualifications, they cannot guarantee you the interview or placement. Getting the job ultimately comes down to your ability to perform and impress at an interview, as well as the dynamics of local politics.

5. Take graduate courses at suburban university campuses where you can develop contacts with aspiring suburban educators and suburban instructors who often work in those districts. Potentially, they can promote your candidacy and provide you with inside information. Working and studying in the city is isolating if your goal is to transition to the "burbs."

### The Resident Candidate

When writing your cover letter, should you mention that you live within the school district, or is it better to leave your residency unsaid? Is your address obvious enough if it is stated on your resume? Can residing in the town or district be held against you? Your address on your resume speaks for itself. Many districts have an unspoken understanding that residents are given a courtesy interview, so you should not read too much into getting an interview. Nevertheless, interviewing is still an opportunity to make a positive impression.

The politics of being a resident can be tricky. In general, board members and parents like the idea of hiring local people. However (although most would ever admit it), such hiring practices make other administrators uncomfortable because residents might allegedly have an "insider's" view on what is really going on and might share that information with community members. Community membership opens up the threat of disloyalty to the leadership team.

You also need to think about your status in the community. Do you have children? How will your role impact them? Is your spouse active in school events? What is the effect? Are you willing to subject yourself and your family to scrutiny whenever you are out in public? These are all important considerations. Let's look at how Julia thinks through her candidacy as a resident candidate.

## Julie Childs—Reflections of a Resident Candidate

*I am a high school Spanish teacher who has been teaching for 11 years in the same district, the first four at the middle school and the rest at the high school. I completed my advanced certificate programs about four years ago. Frankly, I took the program to earn an extra 30 credits, which moved me over to the Masters plus 30 credit lane of the salary schedule. I have not applied for any supervisory positions until I spotted an opening in my home district for a foreign language coordinator.*

*I have a reputation of being a strong teacher. I never have student discipline problems. I stay out of the ongoing and endless dramas and local "political" controversies among and between faculty and administration. That's one of the reasons that I never applied for a supervisory job in the district; I don't like the politics.*

*I've lived in my town for 15 years. My two children attend public school here and are active in the sports and music programs. My husband grew up here. He coaches little league. Although I'm a member of the PTA, I can't say that I've been active. Our family does attend church regularly and I did sing in the choir years ago. My husband and I know several school board members. Our kids are good students and I've never had reason to interact with the school officials here. The school system seems to run smoothly, and folks seem to get along with little conflict. It appears to be a place where I'd like to work.*

*I do feel that I have a lot to share about teaching a foreign language and how to run an effective classroom. My students have always achieved at the highest standards. My background as a Spanish speaker is strong. I took a semester in Spain in my junior year. We've traveled throughout Mexico and Central America over the years. However, I do have some reservations about working in the same town in which we live.*

*I don't want my kids to feel any extra pressure about my working in their schools. I do enjoy a certain amount of anonymity in living here and no one knowing my business. I don't think I'd like to be stopped in the supermarket by parents complaining about their child's teacher or feeling uncomfortable about running errands locally or taking a jog in sweats and a baseball cap, and no makeup. However, I'd cut 30 minutes each way off my commute, and I'm probably looking at an extra $12,000 a year in pay, which we could certainly use for the kids' college fund.*

*I don't like the idea of using political influence by contacting board members and asking them to support me. They know my husband and their kids are friendly with my children, but they don't know me professionally. Finally, I don't think some of the other supervisors would feel comfortable with me. They might think that I got my job through political connections and that I wasn't a loyal member of their leadership team.*

*It's all so much to think about.*

## Dealing with a Layoff, Resignation, or Denial of Tenure

It is devastating to be laid off or asked to resign your position. It can be equally hard to be denied tenure or to resign because you are very unhappy in your job. Needless to say, these actions can represent career-ending events. Leaving a job before getting tenure is a bright red flag. During every interview, you will have to answer the question, "I see you only worked in Happy Hollow for two years. Were you asked to leave? What is the story regarding your leaving?"

Assuming that you were not involved in any serious wrongdoing, be assured that the situation need not be hopeless. (If you committed a serious infraction, then you should find a new line of work.) Once you clear your mind and harness your anxiety, focus and plan your course of action. Effective strategies are available to you. However, let us be clear that however desperate you may feel, you should NEVER LIE. Eventually, every lie tends to be uncovered and you will be terminated for lying, and that would be career damaging or even career ending. Here are some effective strategies to follow instead:

### 1. Get out in front

You may have some control over the timeline. If you are told that you will not be getting tenure, then you are better off resigning. Do whatever you can to get a positive letter of recommendation and a promise that if someone calls for a reference, positive things will be said about you and your work. In turn, promise that you will submit a letter of resignation. Then, do what you can to submit that letter as *late* as possible. Next, start applying as soon as you can. If you are called for interviews, you can honestly say at that point that you have not resigned. Then be prepared to answer the question, "Why do you want to leave?"

## 2. What happens if you resign and you do not have a job?

You need to face the question of why you resigned without hesitation—you cannot appear as if you have something to cover up. You must craft your narrative and be prepared. Practice your response with friends or a coach and always tell the truth. Most leaders have been through career crises and can be very understanding. Just take a breath and briefly tell your story. Your narrative must be credible and evoke empathy. A good coach can help you craft your narrative. Toward the end of the conversation make a brief positive statement beginning with "I'd like to leave you with a final thought." This statement usually makes a powerful last impression. You might say something like "I just want to assure you that I have never done anything I am ashamed of. I am an honorable, hard-working, and sincere person who would never do anything that would discredit or embarrass me or my employer."

## 3. What if you are laid off because of budget cuts?

You will be in a strong position to get excellent letters of recommendation and references. Your supervisors will undoubtedly be sincerely sorry to cut you lose, so do not despair. You are now in a position of being an experienced candidate looking to make a parallel move. Your potential new employer will likely empathize with your situation. If you have a copy of a newspaper article that verifies that your position was lost because of budget cuts, present it at your interview as documentation. It will immediately quell any doubts.

## 4. What if you cannot find a comparable job?

You still have options. You can go back to the classroom. You can explore employment at a private school or charter school. You can seek employment opportunities in a nearby big city. You can relocate. In exploring these opportunities, you might find you could move up the career ladder, from assistant principal to principal, for example.

As a final thought, you should be aware that a career is a marathon, not a sprint. Undergoing a career crisis or transition can be a source of self-growth. You may learn how to be more resilient and discover who your real friends are and how supportive they can be.

## *When Should You Begin Preparing for a Job Search?*

Most candidates don't get serious about their search early enough. They procrastinate right up until the "prime season" for job postings. In general, superintendent searches happen from December through March, Central Office from February to April, principals from April to May, and all other supervisory jobs from March through June. Serious job search preparation includes updating and revising your resume and cover letter, and prepping for interviews. Think of job search preparation as Spring Training. In baseball, Spring Training starts in January in preparation for the regular season that starts in April. The practice of getting ready early makes sense for several reasons.

1. **The odds are in your favor during the "off-season"**—Jobs are posted all year round. Incumbents leave their positions for variety of reasons, such as retirement, childbirth, taking another position, illness and death, relocating, and the necessity of childcare or caring of a loved one. Whereas the number of applicants routinely exceeds hundred during prime season, there may be as few as 20 applicants during off-season. That's a 500 percent advantage. Preparing early means you'll be ready for off-season job postings.

2. **Fine tuning your resume and cover letter takes time**—Crafting your resume requires an ongoing series of revisions and edits over time. The role of the resume is to tell your story in an appealing manner which will distinguish you in a positive way from the rest of the field. To produce a truly effective resume demands meticulous attention to every detail.

3. **The ability to perform an outstanding interview is the result of internalizing thoughtful responses to a range of topics**—I have identified "The 20 Most Asked Interview Questions." The answers to these and other questions cannot and should not be subjected to memorization. A successful candidate needs to create an appealing narrative and to internalize a powerful set of guiding principles that go to the core of the issues. It takes time to marinate a fine steak. Similarly, it takes time to internalize thoughtful answers to interviewers' questions, answer with an authentic voice, and respond efficiently and effectively.

If you are a serious candidate, then take my advice: it is never too soon to prepare yourself. Don't rush the process. Here's what you should do to get started: read how to books, find and meet with a job coach, attend workshops, develop drafts of your resume and cover letter. In summary, preparing early affords you the time to internalize, absorb, develop deeper insights, and marinate your resume and effectively respond to interviewers' questions.

# CHAPTER 2

# GETTING PREPARED

## Resumes and Cover Letters: Effective and Ineffective

Your resume and cover letter are your "calling cards." You cannot proceed to step one—an interview—without your "paperwork" being screened into the *must-see "A Pile."* If you are a well-qualified candidate but are not getting interviews, or if your rate of being called for an interview is low, your resume and cover letter are probably your problem. You need to revise them effectively.

Let us start with the most common mistakes that candidates make. Many candidates try to follow an outdated set of rules that tell you to limit your resume to one page, start your resume with an objective, and follow a strict order of categories such as education, certification, and professional experience. No, no, no.

This is what you should avoid: avoid bullet statements that take the form of a job description; avoid too many bullets; avoid burying your most impressive accomplishments in the text; avoid using small font to squeeze too much on one page; avoid bragging about accomplishments that are irrelevant to the position for which you are applying; avoid typos, avoid weak word selection; avoid grammatical errors, clumsy sentence construction, sentences starting with "I"; avoid using objectives; and avoid the word "very."

Assume that, in today's job market, you are up against 100 other candidates who are also submitting their paperwork. Whoever is screening those hundreds of pages is busy with many other responsibilities. If it takes only two minutes to review each set of paperwork, then a typical review represents about 3½ hours of work for the screener. There is a good chance, then, that your paper will receive less than one minute of attention. The screener will skim the resume. Cover letters often go unread.

Here are some suggestions for constructing a strong resume and cover letter and tailoring them to the position you are seeking:

## 1. Play to your strengths first

Determine what your greatest strengths are relative to the position and put those close to the top of your resume. If you are seeking an entry-level leadership position and do not yet have any significant leadership experience but are a graduate of a prestigious university or hold a doctorate, then list your education first. If you are trying to make a parallel job change, then list your work experience first. If the position calls for being in charge of student discipline, then any experience with disciplining students should go to the top.

## 2. List accomplishments, not a description of your job

Because everyone knows what a math teacher or fourth grade teacher does, why would you provide such a job description on your resume? Your resume must distinguish you from the many other applicants. To that end, you need to identify your accomplishments precisely and powerfully. If, when you started teaching an AP course, the percentage of students passing went from 30 percent to 80 percent that is a significant accomplishment if you are applying for a subject area coordinator's job. If as a dean of discipline you developed a data-driven process that identified "hot spots and times" of fist fights, and student suspensions consequently decreased by 30 percent, put that proudly at the top of your bulleted list if you are applying for an assistant principal position. Quantify your accomplishments whenever possible.

## 3. Research the problems of the school and/or the school system you have chosen and present yourself as the solution to their problems

Napoleon once said you can never spend too much time doing surveillance. You need to do deep research into the school, the district, and its leaders. Identify their problems and then craft your paperwork to conspicuously cast yourself as the kind of leader who can solve their problems. Assume that you learn that the school has serious teacher morale problems. That should encourage you to mention your service as the PTA teacher representative and cochairperson of the annual teacher recognition luncheon. Such experiences should appear near the top of your bullet statements.

Here are a few final thoughts. Never fictionalize or inflate your credentials or accomplishments. In education, there are only a few degrees of separation between your past experiences and your new one. Falsifying the details on your resume can lead to dismissal. Be aware that you are too close to your own paperwork to be objective. Ask an informed and respected mentor, colleague, or coach to review your paperwork and give you objective feedback. Your resume and cover letter are works in progress. Continuously revise them depending on the feedback, the uniqueness of the position for which you are applying, and your results as measured by the number of interviews you receive and the feedback that you might get.

## Words and Phrases Never to be Used on Your Resume or in an Interview

Here is a list of words and phrases you never want to use on your resume or during an interview. Why you shouldn't use them? And what to say instead.

1. "UNEMPLOYED"—It makes you sound like a loser and nobody wants to hire a loser. Let potential employers figure out that you are "between jobs" and be prepared to explain what happened.
2. "HARDWORKING"—The word is overused and therefore trite. Instead, provide accomplishments that document your work ethic and diligence and let the interviewer infer that you're hardworking.
3. "AMBITIOUS"—Making personality claims comes off as bragging. You want to project a modest image which is backed up by progressive accomplishments and activities.
4. "OBJECTIVE"—Stating your career object at the top of your resume is superfluous. It is clear what position you are applying for. Stating an objective in flowery language only slows the reviewer down. He/she is probably speed reading through 100's of resumes. Just leave it out.
5. "DEDICATED"—This is another overused, stale personal claim. Describe your passions and your actions over a period of time to fulfill them.
6. "UNION"—Remember that unions often sit on the other side of the table pushing back on leaders' decisions and actions. Leaders make personnel decisions and may not welcome people who are "union-friendly" on their team. Leave out any mention of unions.
7. "LIFELONG LEARNER"—Another trite expression. Your ongoing participation in professional development opportunities demonstrates your willingness to learn and grow. During the interview, ask about professional development opportunities and who would be mentoring you. That question implies that you want to grow and learn.

8. "ROCK STAR"—No one likes a braggart. You're not Elvis, Justin Bieber, or Lady Gaga.

9. "DABBLED"—Either you know or did something significant about something that is important enough to mention. Who wants to hire a dabbler? Use strong verbs like led, created, and directed.

10. "EXPERT"—Be careful what you claim. A skillful interviewer may probe or challenge your expertise. "What does the research say on the topic of [...]? What research and literature have you studied?" If you claim to speak a foreign language, don't be surprised if an interviewer asks you a complex question in that language and asks that you respond in that language.

11. "A BIG FAN OF [...]"—Speak like a professional. I'm a big baseball fan, however I wouldn't tell a group of professions that I was a big fan of differentiating instruction. I would describe how I go about differentiating.

12. "LIKE"—Using the words "like" or "you know" at the beginning, the middle, and the end of every sentence as a "filler" makes you sound juvenile and will hamper your professional image. Work to change that speech pattern.

These are just a few examples of words and phrases to avoid. There are many others. I would also caution you about referencing anything related to politics and religion, or what might be perceived as controversial topics. Needless to say, never use any words even bordering on profanity. Everything you write and say as a candidate creates your narrative and your image. Choose your words carefully.

## Verbs to Use on Your Resume

Resumes require descriptive and active verbs to make reviewers fully aware of your accomplishments, knowledge, skills, and dispositions. I have lifted many of the actual verbs that my clients have used in their resumes. Some are better than others although they may connote similar meanings. To my thinking, the more active the verb the better. As an example, "develop" is neutral compared to "create"; "inspire" has a more positive emotional component compared to "motivate."

Here are many examples to choose from. I'm sure there are others. However, you should find these examples very useful in crafting your resume.

| | |
|---|---|
| 1. OVERSEE | 26. CONTROL |
| 2. DIRECT | 27. GOVERN |
| 3. SUPERVISE | 28. STIMULATE |
| 4. MANAGE | 29. KINDLE |
| 5. RUN | 30. ADVANCE |
| 6. ADMINISTER | 31. USE |
| 7. CREATE | 32. DESIGN |
| 8. DEVELOP | 33. CRAFT |
| 9. ADVANCE | 34. INSTRUCT |
| 10. BRING ABOUT | 35. TEACH |
| 11. COACH | 36. MENTOR |
| 12. NURTURE | 37. GUIDE |
| 13. ACCOMPLISH | 38. PLAN |
| 14. ENHANCE | 39. STRATEGIZE |
| 15. INCREASE | 40. PROPOSE |
| 16. GROW | 41. PROVIDE LEADERSHIP |
| 17. ENCOURAGE | 42. WRITE |
| 18. FOSTER | 43. AUTHOR |
| 19. INSPIRE | 44. FOUNDER OF |
| 20. MOTIVATE | 45. INITIATE |
| 21. PERSUADE | 46. RECRUIT |
| 22. CONVINCE | 47. REFORM |
| 23. INFLUENCE | 48. SYNTHISIZE |
| 24. SUPPORT | 49. ANALYZE |
| 25. SUSTAIN | 50. FORMED |

## What Are They Really Looking For?

You may find yourself asking: Why am I not getting interviews, and when I do, why aren't districts calling me back for the next interview? To better understand how you get your leadership job, you need to better understand what the employers are *really* seeking. Your qualifications and experience are only a part of their search agenda. What *are* they looking for?

In no particular order, here is my analysis: (1) fit, (2) judgment, (3) know-how, (4) work ethic, (5) commitment, (6) loyalty, (7) team player, (8) intelligence, (9) professionalism, and (10) low maintenance.

How do you, as a candidate, communicate how you fulfill each of these criteria? Be aware that few screeners or interviewing committees ever actually explicitly articulate these criteria. When you read the job postings, you will rarely find most of these qualities listed. If districts did post such an ad, it might read like this (tongue in cheek):

> The Happy Hollow School District is seeking candidates who will fit into our quirky school community, not rock the boat, know when to keep their mouths shut, show up every night to every community function, and not make demands on us.

These unwritten criteria are implicit and intuitive. The candidate's narrative—that is, your resume, cover letter, responses to interview questions—all need to be delicately crafted to address these criteria. How you successfully do this as a candidate makes all the difference.

Each school–community is unique. Even the schools within a district are different. As a consequence, you need to gather as much information in advance on the nature of the district, the neighborhood, the school leaders, the political landscape, their strengths and needs, their biases, and their recent and not-so-recent history.

With the information you gather, you are better prepared to paint a detailed picture of yourself. However, bear in mind that you will never have a complete understanding of the school and community until you actually work there. Another caution: do not present yourself as someone you are not. In other words, do not lie or misrepresent who you are. It becomes a matter of emphasizing the genuine and observable qualities, skills, knowledge, and values that you hold.

Here are suggestions you might incorporate into your written and spoken narrative:

## 1. Fit

Emphasize those aspects of your family and personal background that match the values of the community. Say such statements as "I think my colleagues would describe me as someone who is easy to get along with" or "If I'm fortunate enough to get this position, you will find that I'll be a visible presence throughout the community."

## 2. Judgment

Make clear that you are thorough, that you gather as much relevant information as you can before making decisions, and that you actively seek and welcome the advice of other experienced leaders.

### 3. Know-how

Let them know about the skill sets you have developed. Such skills as scheduling, use of technology, designing professional development sessions, school safety, and involvement in athletics are all valuable areas that demonstrate know-how.

### 4. Work Ethic

How is this for an admirable work ethic? "I think you'll find that I'll be one of the first to arrive in the morning and the last to leave after school. You'll find me at athletic and other extra-curricular activities. My father taught me that you give a full day's work for a full day's pay."

### 5. Commitment

Commitment is ideally measured by time, space, energy, and passion. The powers-that-be want to hear that you will stay with them for at least five to seven years; that you live nearby, preferably in the community, or would consider moving into the district; that you will devote your time above and beyond the school day to the interests of your students, the parents, and the school; and that you really want this job because you respect and value everything you have come to know about the district and its people. You need to be specific and sincere in each assertion.

### 6. Loyalty

When I encounter someone, who speaks ill of others, I assume that he or she will probably, at some point, speak ill of me as well. Therefore, never be critical of your present or past employers, supervisors, or communities. I am always grateful for the opportunities that my past associates afforded me and the important lessons I learned while working with them. If you are asked to comment on your former place of work, and it might even be common knowledge that it is a troubled place, do not be critical. You might say, "It would be unprofessional of me to criticize a former employer. And in the same way, you can be sure that I would never be critical of you."

### 7. Collaborative

Being a team player means that you play well with others. You are willing to take one for the team. You pass the ball to the open player so that he or she can score. You praise others and give credit to deserving colleagues. You make every effort to contribute to the team's success. All of this is conveyed implicitly through your narrative.

## 8. Intelligence

Intelligent people think before they speak, present coherent and purposeful ideas, and link ideas that are grounded in good research and based on implications derived from data. Moreover, intelligent people are practical. A good candidate demonstrates intelligence by briefly pausing before responding to a thoughtful question and briefly providing a rationale upon which the response is based. Such rationales should be your "guiding principles."

## 9. Professionalism

An interview is like a stage play: the casting director is looking for an actor who looks and sounds professional—in this case, a leader. I am impressed with people who present themselves as self-confident and behave like adults; people who look like a professional and speak like an adult. Stay away from inserting "like" into every sentence. Every sentence deserves a subject and a verb and should not end with "you know." Dress for the part: men should wear a business suit with shined shoes and tasteful tie, and women should dress modestly with toned-down jewelry and makeup.

## 10. Low Maintenance

Leave your baggage at home. Refrain from complaining about anybody or anything. Nobody likes a complainer or whiner. Keep your personal problems out of the conversation (even if you just went through a difficult divorce, your mother is seriously ill, or your husband is unemployed). This advice also applies while being in the actual job. Educators by nature are compassionate and caring. However, even we have limits. Dealing with high-maintenance people is draining and distracts from the mission of educating students.

## Assistant Principal Job: What Does the Principal Really Need?

Oftentimes, the entry-level job into school leadership is the assistant principalship. There are more assistant principal jobs than any other leadership roles. At this moment there are 13 positions being posted on Long Island. During the selection process, the principal is usually the key person in deciding who will get the job. The fact is that the assistant will be the principal's right arm. What does the principal *really* need?

In my experience, despite what the job description says, principals need an assistant who can do *six* things. They are: (1) student discipline; (2) observations and evaluations; (3) large group supervision (bus duty, cafeteria duty, corridors); (4) parent complaints; (5) teacher supervision; (6) scheduling. These responsibilities may not be very glamorous, but they are essential in assuring that the school is well organized, safe, and orderly.

Of the six responsibilities, *student discipline* by far is the highest priority. Realistically, the assistant principal's school day is dominated by dealing with time-consuming disciplinary cases, mostly routine but sometimes more serious. Therefore, the principal is looking for an assistant principal who exercises good judgment, is thorough, is effective with kids, and knows how to speak with parents in a tactful and respectful manner.

The ability to command respect by just being a presence is vital; some call it "gravitas." That is the ability to project self-confidence, influence, credibility, and command respect. When you speak, others listen. In order to be an effective supervisor in large group settings, and in dealing with staff or parents, it is a requirement to project gravitas.

You should assume that the reviewer of your resume and your interviewers, and particularly the principal, will be looking for evidence that you have some experience, knowledge, and skills in fulfilling most of these six responsibilities. Be aware that these "top six" needs do not include such areas as professional development, curriculum development, personnel or budget management among others, even though these functions might be included in the job description. The principal is going to choose a candidate based on what he/she needs and not what's wanted.

Your resume should prominently include evidence of performing these six functions, and you should prepare answers to interviewers' questions pertaining to these areas. Expect "what would you do" scenarios that are aimed at assessing your judgment and practical knowledge of how these various processes work. A few sample questions might be:

1. Walk us through step-by-step how you would deal with a fight in the corridor?
2. Role-playing the assistant principal who receives a phone call from an irate parent complaining that his child is being treated unfairly by a teacher.

3. How would you deal with a veteran teacher who is not addressing recommendations you made on his/her observation report?
4. How would you go about doing a formal teacher observation?

The key to be a successful candidate is preparation. Focus your preparation on the real priorities of the person to whom you'll be assisting.

# CHAPTER 3

# EXECUTING YOUR STRATEGIES

## Getting Interviews: Debunking Myths

How do districts really screen and select prospective candidates for interviews? The process seems mysterious. Debunking the unknown can better illuminate what actually happens and how you might make it work to your advantage. Each district customizes its process; however, the variations are usually minor. How does it really work?

The process all starts with the posting. The human resources administrator is usually the person who writes and distributes the posting. He or she may run it by someone who will supervise the new hire for his or her input. Thus, it is important to carefully review the job description and qualifications that appear in the posting and modify and tailor your resume and letter of application to best address these requirements. The posting can be distributed in several ways: (1) internal distribution only, (2) an online system like OLAS (Online Application System), (3) a newspaper advertisement, and/or (4) professional organization newsletters and online systems. An exclusive internal posting means that the local educational leaders are looking only at internal candidates and might already have some people in mind already. A newspaper ad is very expensive. This sort of advertising usually indicates that the district is serious about attracting highly qualified applicants. The online system is now the usual approach of choice because it is quick, easy, versatile, and inexpensive. You must register with the relevant online systems and keep your credentials updated. You also should replace your letter and resume for each application when appropriate—don't be lazy!

If you are an internal candidate, you should go through the same application process as everyone else. If a potential employer is interested in you, someone may confidentially reach out and encourage your application. This encouragement may come indirectly, through a messenger. If you are encouraged, keep it to yourself. Though you may feel flattered, confide in no one.

Filling a leadership position can be highly political; speculation is the sport of the day. The supervisor can be embarrassed to find out that others think he or she was playing favorites. In addition, if you or your supervisors have detractors and they have early warning that you are a candidate, this gives them time to launch a campaign to stop you. Although his is sad, but it can be a reality.

An affluent district with a good reputation will attract many more qualified candidates than a poorly financed district which might also have a history of conflict. Whatever the case, the screening process always becomes a numbers game. Let us assume there is a vacancy for an assistant principal which comes up on OLAS, a popular New York State online site; each state has something similar. Assume that the reputable district receives 150 applicants and the lesser reputable district receives 30. There is a continuum, ranging from the most to least attractive places which is generally proportional to the number of applicants.

Then, you apply for the position and wait patiently. Do not be a pest and call the personnel office to inquire about your status. The human resources personnel are always busy filling many different positions and trying to resolve difficult issues. Some directors of human resources will quickly screen the resumes as they accumulate online. My experience is that about 10–15 percent of the applicants are unqualified because they do not meet the minimum qualifications regarding certification, education, and experience. My practice is to have the personnel office staff print out the letters and resumes of all qualified candidates and send them to the direct supervisor for paper screening. How is the paperwork screened? What is the screener looking for? How many applicants make it through to the interviewing committee? How is the committee selected? How does the interviewing committee make decisions?

The personnel officer will send the pile of resumes and letters to the direct supervisor. Let's say, after eliminating the unqualified there are now 100 qualified applicants remaining in the pile. The plan is to convene an initial screening committee of two or three people and have them interview 15–18 candidates. How do the personnel officers get from 100 to 15 using only the paperwork? If it takes two minutes to review each candidate's papers, that's 200 minutes or more than three hours. It is a sad reality that each candidate's papers usually will receive less than two minutes of attention.

As a consequence, the reviewer will generally scan the resumes. At this point in the process, the letter of application will not receive much scrutiny. However, a wise note of caution: any typos and grammatical errors might well lead your application to be immediately eliminated. A frequent error is to receive a letter addressed to another district's administrator. Such errors connote that you are sloppy and make mistakes.

Now how does the paper screener use those two minutes? His or her goal is usually to sort the total pile into three piles. Pile A will contain the "must see" candidate, B the "maybe" candidates, and C "of no further interest" candidates. Individuals who reach the A group are those who (1) are making a "good" parallel move, (2) hold degrees from outstanding universities, (3) hold a doctorate, (4) are qualified internal candidates or courtesy interviews, and (5) are exceptional and/or interesting candidates. The B pile is created in case the reviewers cannot place 15–18 into the A pile. In that case, the B documents will receive a second look. The C pile is composed of applications from inexperienced people who have fewer accomplishments and poor reputations, seem to be "perennial" candidates, or evidence inexplicable and suspicious gaps on their resumes.

A "good" parallel move occurs when you have earned tenure in your present position, when you are seeking to move into a better district that may pay more, or when the move represents a significantly shorter commute. Unfortunately, if you have not received tenure after four years or you are leaving before completing four years, your leaving is not a "good" parallel move unless you have been laid off because of budget cuts or some kind of legitimate reorganization.

Outstanding universities tend to be the Ivy League schools or other prestigious schools familiar to all of us. For example, in the New York area, graduate degrees from Columbia University Teachers College, New York University, and Fordham University are the most coveted. Undergraduate degrees from fine colleges are also appealing on resumes. I always counsel aspiring leaders who are serious about their careers in leadership to earn their doctorate from a prestigious university. It is an investment in yourself that will likely assure your placement in A pile and it will save you years of disappointment as you apply for positions that result in coming up empty. Unfortunately, the tuitions to such colleges are high and the commute might be longer, but ultimately the investment will pay off.

Exceptional and/or interesting candidates come in different forms: they have been successful in the business and corporate world, the nonprofit sector, entrepreneurship, or the military. When qualified, these candidates, depending on their accomplishments, are often worthy of a good look. Finally, courtesy interviews are given to those who have "friends in high places," such as board members and upper-level administrators. A courtesy interviewee is generally guaranteed a screening interview only. After the screening interview, the candidate is on his or her own and must compete fairly with everyone else.

The screening interview usually takes 10–20 minutes, rarely more. Since the pandemic these interviews are frequently done virtually. You might also be required to send a five-minute video in which you introduce yourself and answer a question. If you are told that an interview will take 10–20 minutes but lasts longer, that is a good sign—it shows interest. In-person appointments never run on time, so arrive a few minutes early and expect to wait a while. You will probably find yourself in an area near a receptionist. If the interviews are running very late, you will encounter other candidates waiting there as well. Remember that you are not in the waiting area to make friends with other candidates; but, try to be friendly to the receptionist. If you have the receptionist to yourself, try to engage with him or her. Information is power. You might find out how late the interviews are running, how many candidates are being seen, how long the interviews have been lasting, and who is conducting the interviews. If the receptionist is reluctant to engage, then do not push the conversation. However, receptionists are often bored with their job routines and might enjoy the attention. In any event, someone will eventually invite you into the interview room. Smile, shake hands, be friendly. Your escort will try to make you feel at ease by cordially asking something like, "Did you find us without any problems?" or "Is it still raining?" or "How long have you been waiting?"

The screening committee will likely consist of two or three people. Assuming that you are interviewing for an assistant principal position, you will probably meet the principal, an assistant principal, perhaps the director of human resources, and/or a teacher. Be aware that the screening interview is essentially a "beauty contest." It is designed to see if you are a "regular person" (not quirky, odd, or inappropriate), likeable, well-spoken, professional, intelligent, easy to engage, respectful, and a good fit for the community.

Interviewers usually start by asking you to say something about yourself. Interviewees usually respond by walking through their work experiences. I advise my clients to be different. The interviewers already have your resume in front of them.

Be prepared to answer what I call resume questions. "You've been an assistant principal at the ABC School for four years. Why do you want to leave now?" "I understand that your school recently hired a new principal. Were you a candidate for that position?" "I see you were a dean for two years and then you went back to the classroom. Can you explain this?" The interviewers may also ask what I call process or "how would you?" questions: "Walk us through how you would observe a teacher who is not in your area of teacher certification." Limit your answers to no more than two minutes. If they want more, they will ask for it.

The moderator will wrap up the interview by saying something like, "We're speaking to a number of folks. Hopefully, we'll be back to you within the next couple of weeks one way or another. Do you have any questions for us at this time?" Now remember, the committee is under strict time constraints. They are just being polite and really do not want to answer many questions. Recognize that it is time to thank them for the opportunity, indicate that you look forward to seeing them again, and leave them with an upbeat thought— "I just want you to know that I am the real thing. I'm a hard worker and take all of my professional responsibilities very seriously." With that, you will be escorted out.

Upon completing their 15 interviews, the committee members will review their options. Their goal is to reduce the queue of candidates to a reasonable number of six to eight. I always leave a few minutes between interviews for committee members to share their impressions and debrief. A good moderator might start off with, "Let's see if we can reach agreement on who we can eliminate." Given those short feedback discussions between the interviews, this step is often easy. "Do we have consensus on eliminating candidate B? Okay, how about F?" Often, we can quickly boil the list down to about ten candidates. Next, the moderator might ask, "Who would like to propose cutting additional people?" This step usually takes a bit longer, but ultimately the committee screens the group down to six to eight and completes its job. The next step is for the semifinalists to proceed to the larger interviewing committee.

Immediately after your interview, send a warm one-paragraph thank-you email or note to the moderator. While this will not be a game changer, your choice not to send a note might leave a negative impression. In any event, do not call anyone as you do not want to be perceived as a pest. The time has arrived to wait it out and hope for the best. If you are rejected and the moderator appeared to be sincerely approachable, you might want to write a short email thanking him or her for the professionalism with which you were treated and asking if it would be okay to schedule a brief telephone conversation to obtain constructive feedback. Do not be disappointed if they do not reply, but if they do, you will get valuable feedback for self-reflection.

My experience is that good news travels by phone or a text, and bad news comes in the form of a letter or an email. Let's hope your phone always rings!

### Be Likeable

The *most* important factor during an interview is likeability. Likeability can trump your knowledge of pedagogy, your qualifications—in short, almost everything. Interviewers often decide within the first few minutes whether or not they like you. Still, over the course of the interview, interviewers can change their opinions in either direction. If they really like you, they may even over-look your less-than-satisfactory responses to some questions. So, what can you do to help them like you?

To determine how to be more likeable, let's first ask, "What is it that makes me like someone whom I first meet?" I like people who are friendly, smile, relaxed, well-groomed, modest, pleasant, sincere, respectful, and moderate. Moreover, we probably like people who enjoy good humor and resonate with our values. Of course, there are also uncontrollable elements, such as a resemblance to a highly respected friend or colleague. Unfortunately, we cannot control the uncontrollable, but here are a few suggestions for what you can control:

1. Smile.
2. Dress appropriately and modestly—it is equally important to not over-dress as it is to not underdress. Limit jewelry to a small number of modest pieces. Hair styles should be simple and appropriate. Going on an inter-view is not going on a date.
3. Shake hands with everyone, look each person in the eye, smile, and tell the interviewers your name. The warm firm human touch and proximity of person-to-person contact are magical.
4. Pay attention to nonverbal cues. Sit up, lean forward, make eye contact with a speaker, acknowledge your understanding by nodding and smil-ing, and acknowledge others' nods and smiles by nodding and smiling in return. Do not cross your arms. Do not shake your head from side to side or grimace in disagreement or disapproval.
5. Laugh appropriately. If someone says something funny, it is appropriate to laugh, but do not overdo it. It is also good to slip in a humorous remark within the context of the interaction, but keep in mind you are not there to entertain. If you are the only one laughing and joking, it is a wise idea to stop!
6. Shake hands at the conclusion of the interview. Smile and thank each person.

Before walking into the room for your interview, your mantra should be "Be likeable. Be likeable!"

### *Overcoming Nervousness*

"I get so nervous when I interview that I freeze." For most of us, interviewing is an unfamiliar, somewhat intimidating, and uncomfortable experience. It is natural that interviewees feel nervous. There's a lot at stake. You have invested a great deal of time, effort, and money in trying to take the next step in your career. You're walking into a room all alone to meet a group of strangers who are going to ask you difficult questions and make judgments whether they like you, if you're a good fit, and as to your qualifications and readiness. Feelings of rejection are a real possibility. So, what do you do to calm your nerves and become more effective?

You should take some comfort in knowing that the interviewers who are seated across the table have also been on your side of the table and understand your nervousness. They are quite forgiving of a shaky voice and a little perspiration. But how do you avoid freezing? My formula for shedding your nervousness is as follows:

(1) Be familiar with each step of the interview process so that there are no unnerving surprises;

(2) Be prepared by anticipating many of the questions and practicing your answers;

(3) Learn how to read and respond to the interviewers' body language and nonverbal clues;

(4) Find comfort in knowing that your knowledge and skillfulness are well developed;

(5) Stay out of "your own head" (how am I doing; are they liking me) by just focusing on answering the question;

(6) Direct your response to the individual who asked the question (avoid looking at the large group);

(7) Plant seeds in your answers that will lead the interviewers to ask a follow-up question for which you will be well prepared, thus gaining some control over the direction of the course of the interview.

Perhaps an analogous situation might serve to illustrate my approach. I must confess that sometimes I get anxious when I travel. I imagine that the taxi is going to drop me at the wrong terminal; the flight will be overbooked and I'll get bumped; the plane will leave late and I'll miss my connecting flight; upon arrival I'll be told that my hotel reservation was for last week and they are now all booked up. However, I'm happy to report that over time I have figured out ways to alleviate most of my anxieties. I take a page from my own formula. I familiarize myself in advance with my ticket which identifies the terminal; I try to book nonstop direct flights; I reconfirm my hotel reservation; and if unanticipated problems arise, I have copies of all the documentation and contact phone numbers in my possession—you get the idea.

A good coach will walk you through the interview process step-by-step. You will learn what forms of body language to look for and how you should respond verbally and nonverbally. You will analyze and practice answering the most often asked questions. You will role-play and have a dress rehearsal. You will report back to your coach as to your actual performance and get feedback on how you might improve. You will find comfort and self-confidence in the knowledge that you are well prepared, and as a result your nervousness will be minimized.

## *Body Language*

It has been said that 90 percent of what we communicate is expressed through body language. Body language is interactive, a two-way street between the candidate and the interviewers as well as among the interviewers. An effective candidate must be disciplined to be aware of and control his or her own body language, and observe, interpret, and respond to the body language of the interviewers.

I learned the importance of my body language the hard way. I was interviewed by a small group of consultants who worked for a prominent search firm. They were very friendly and nodded their approval to my responses throughout the hour-long interview. I became relaxed, sat back in my seat, crossed my legs (which are a little long), and balanced the edge of my knee on the corner of the table which separated us. I left the interview feeling I had aced it and was confident I would be called back as a finalist. That did not happen.

How could I have misjudged my performance so badly? I returned to my mentor with a sense of defeat and we reviewed my performance. Because I was not aware of my body language during the interview, I did not report on that parameter. My mentor could not diagnose any deficiencies either. However, he did know a couple of the search consultants and promised to get their feedback the next time he saw them. Several months passed before my mentor got the feedback.

"You're not going to believe the feedback," he reported. "They loved your answers. But one of the guys noticed that you were too relaxed. He said you sat back and even put your knee on the edge of the table. He felt you were cocky."

About a year passed. There I was again interviewing with the same group of search consultants. Needless to say, I leaned forward this time. No sitting back for me. I moved on in the process and actually got that job.

My advice concerning body language is to lean forward in your seat. Slowly scan the faces and eyes of all the interviewers. If they like what you are saying, they will usually nod and smile. Nod back subtly. Focus on the people who are not giving nonverbal feedback. Watch to see if they give knowing looks to one another. Often, you might say something that resonates with an issue they have previously discussed. A glance, a smile, a nod, a shake of the head between interviewers means you may have confirmed or disagreed with something of interest to them. A shake of the head probably means that you have stepped on an explosive device. Quickly backtrack and clarify your statement, if you can, to neutralize the potential damage.

Researchers in the field of body language report that your ability to subtly mimic other people's gestures and postures indicates you are in sync with them. If someone leans forward, lean toward him or her. If someone smiles and nods, then smile and nod back. All your actions must be subtle. Practice mimicking at meetings and social gatherings. You will find it effective in gaining approval.

### Does the Order in Which You Interview Matter?

"Congratulations! You have been selected to be interviewed for the assistant principal position at the Happy Hollow Public Schools. This is Dr. Buggerband's secretary. I'd like to schedule an appointment."

Of course, you are thrilled. Barely able to breathe, you reply, "Yes, I'd be delighted!" The secretary says in an almost mechanical voice, "How about next Wednesday at 4:30 at the Middle School? I can email a confirmation that will include directions." You immediately accept the appointment.

You think, "I've got to tell my spouse."

Your spouse is elated as well, but then asks, "How many people are being interviewed? Who will interview you? How long will it last? Do you have to bring anything with you?"

Feeling a little deflated, you answer, "I don't know."

Does the order in which you interview really matter? My answer is yes. Admittedly, I do not have any research to back up my theory, but I do have more than 40 years' experience of interviewing and being interviewed. Call it empirical data. My theory depends on how many people are being interviewed.

- In a large field of candidates—a number more than five—you want to go last or get toward the rear of the line.
- In a small field of candidates—between three and five—you want to go first or get to the front of the line.
- If the list is down to two or three candidates, then the order is irrelevant.

What's the logic? If you met 18 people for 15 minutes each over a six-hour period, who would you remember best? The screening committee is made up of real people. Despite their best efforts, they get fatigued and bored. Most candidates appear to be mediocre and the exercise becomes a bit of a blur. After a few hours, the panelists look back at the list of names and cannot remember most of the faces. Some of the memorable folks are remembered for negative reasons. The panelists are dying to see a candidate they can love. Here comes number 17 or 18—finally, a really good candidate. Through contrast alone, the value of number 18 swells to epic proportions, sometimes even beyond the reality.

Now let us visit the Central Office interview. The interviewers are seeing four semifinalists, all of whom they can readily remember. The first candidate does a great job. This candidate's performance becomes the "high-water mark," the front-runner. The rest of the field has the challenge of measuring up. By the time the interviewers get to candidate four, the performance of number one has become exaggerated in their minds.

If my theory makes sense to you, then how will you know how many are in the field, how long the interviews will last, and who will do the interviewing? More importantly, how will you obtain that last or first spot? Let's examine the following scenario to see how.

Dr. Buggerband's secretary, who schedules the interviews, sets up hundreds of interviews for a wide range of positions. In this case, her boss gives her a stack of 18 resumes and tasks her to set up interviews every 20 minutes, beginning at 3:30 p.m. and finishing at 6:00 p.m. That amounts to seven interviews on Tuesday and Wednesday, and four on Thursday. She also sends emails to the three members of the screening committee, confirming their participation.

Scheduling a round of interviews is routine business for the secretary. This is how you can get the appointment and the information you want.

*Secretary (S):* "Hello. I'm calling from the Happy Hollow Public Schools. I'd like to schedule a screening interview for the assistant principal position for which you applied. How about next Wednesday at 3:50 at the Middle School?"

*Candidate (C):* "Wonderful. Gee, that's a little tight. What other times are available?"

*S:* "Okay, I have Tuesday at 4:30 and 5:30, Wednesday at 3:30 and 5:30, and a couple of spots on Thursday."

So, what can we derive from this? It looks like there's three days of interviewing. It appears that each interview will be 20 minutes. I might guess the last interview runs from 5:30 to 5:50 p.m. and the committee will be out before dinner time. In addition, Thursday is the last day.

*C:* "What's the latest time you have available on Thursday?"

*S:* "I have 4:10 on Thursday."

*C:* "Great, I'll take it. Can you tell me with whom I'll be meeting?"

*S:* "There are three people on the committee. There will be a teacher and the middle school principal."

*C:* "Thanks so much. I'm really excited."

*S:* "You're welcome. I'll be sending you a confirmation that will include directions. Good luck."

You have the next-to-last spot. There are 18 candidates and the interviews run 20 minutes. You know the size and composition of the screening committee. That's how it's done!

### Gathering Information

Information is power. You will likely be asked what you know about the school–community. You have at your disposal many ways to gather this information. Most candidates will check out the school's and district's website and achievement test data. Networking would be near the top of the list. Speak with friends and colleagues, and friends of friends—folks who work and/or live in the target district. Remember, you are collecting opinions, and beauty is in the eyes of the beholder. Therefore, attempt to get as many diverse reliable sources as you can. Read the local newspaper stories; most towns have weekly newspapers online. Read the comments, editorials, and letters to the editor. Also, drive through the district. Check out the condition and location of the school(s); stop into a local supermarket, pizza place, and public library (libraries have a collection of local newspapers). Drive around the neighborhood of the school. Get an idea of the condition of the homes and apartments, and availability of parks, libraries, places of worship, shopping, and community centers. All these avenues provide insightful information.

You might consider even going so far as checking out the local real estate listings to get a sense of property values. Attend a few open houses and speak to the realtors about the neighborhood and schools. Attend a sports event or concert. Develop an intuition about the community. Unless it is a very small community, you will be anonymous and unmemorable as you make your way around.

Your response to the query, "What do you know about us?" must be positive. Most community leaders love their schools and community and do not appreciate an "outsider" being critical. This is similar to growing your own tomatoes in your garden. You spend significant time nurturing your garden and are proud of your tomatoes. So, when you serve a guest your salad and ask, "What do you think of my tomatoes?" you don't want the guest to criticize them. Likewise, in an interview, you must be diplomatic. The interviewers are neither seeking constructive criticism nor are you there to serve as their consultant.

However, if the interviewers indicate their displeasure with an aspect of the school (low test scores, high rate of student lateness's, high teacher absenteeism), then you might comment on their criticisms with what you found in your information gathering.

Sometimes, a follow-up question from an interviewer might be, "What did you do in order to learn more about us?" Do not hesitate to share your resourcefulness with them. They will likely be impressed by your resourcefulness in thoroughly researching their district. I would suggest leaving out the visits to open houses! Also, keep the identities of your sources confidential as it is unprofessional to reveal names.

### Projecting Your Gravitas: A Key to Winning the Job

I've coached hundreds of school leaders and teachers about the importance of presenting oneself in a confident manner during an interview. This is called "gravitas"; that is the ability to project self-confidence, influence, credibility, and command respect. When you speak, do others listen? Do not confuse gravitas with arrogance. People who project gravitas should also be thoughtful; they think before they speak and enhance the conversation by adding to it. Be mindful that the court jester never becomes the king or the queen.

In seeking a position as a school leader or a teacher, you must convince your potential supervisors that you are the kind of person who brings a certain bearing to the position. The teacher represents the adult leader in the classroom. In the context of a job interview, here are several methods to project your gravitas:

#### 1. Be present, listen, and speak once you've formulated a response

People with gravitas are attentive to the core of the interviewers' questions, the underlying issues and agendas. So, during an interview, take a moment to formulate a thoughtful and relevant response, and draw upon your self-assurance that your response will have value. This can be done quietly without trying to show off that you're the smartest person that they will interview. Be respectful of the people around the table who may be more accomplished and experienced than you. But be confident that your thoughts have value too.

## 2. Demonstrate deep understanding

Your challenge is to put forth relevant information and ideas that demonstrate deep insight. Someone who is self-confident and secure treats everyone with respect, even some panelists who might challenge your answers and might not treat you with respect. Never appear combative or show irritation.

Remember the lyrics to the old song, "You're got to know when to hold 'em, know when to fold 'em." Be mindful about timing what to say, when to say it, and what not to say. Try to make your ideas concise, on point, and clear. Don't repeat yourself. Only when necessary, ask questions to clarify what is being asked, but keep answers on topic, and avoid providing a long context and introductions to your answers. Do not view questions as "gotcha" opportunities. Your goal should be to try to guide the process in productive directions.

## 3. Communicate like an adult

As an employer, I want to hire professionals—adults. People with gravitas speak like adults. Too many young people saturate their sentences with word fillers and phrases such as "like," "you know," "at the end of the day," "to be honest," and "in reference to." You know what I mean! Also, avoid ending your sentences with an upward inflection to your voice as if you're asking a question rather than making a statement. You want to be taken seriously. Therefore, you cannot just dress and look like a professional, you must also sound like a professional.

## 4. Do not confuse confidence with arrogance

There is a thin line separating arrogance and gravitas. Arrogance means that you're perceived as coming across as overbearing, conceited, a know it all, someone who has a lot to say but really offers little in the way of substance. Most of us are repelled by arrogance in others. To me, the opposite of arrogance is modesty. Oftentimes, less is more. We admire wisdom. I once asked an extremely successful businessperson about his newest venture. He described his new business in one sentence. I commented, "You did that in one sentence." He smiled politely and responded, "If you can't explain something in one sentence, then you don't understand what you're talking about." That's gravitas.

### 5. Monitor yourself

How are my responses being received? Is my audience hearing me? Are they resonating with my ideas? Are they nodding and smiling? Exercising your gravitas is not a trick—it's a matter of being effective. When gravitas is lacking, people notice, and when it's there, it's magic.

When you walk away from the table, you want your audience to say, "That candidate really held our attention and was most impressive."

## Take a Risk

A client recently asked me, "How do you respond to the question, 'Why do you want to be an assistant principal?'" If this represents an entry-level leadership job and you are now serving as a teacher, your response may be:

> The principal needs all the help he or she can get. I can only imagine the pressures of their job. As an assistant, my role is to support my principal in every way possible. I'm a team player, and I know how to be a back-up person. In my graduate studies and internship, I learned new skills and gained new knowledge and insights as to leadership. I just need an opportunity to put all of this to work. I know how the job of being an assistant principal should *not* be done. But I also believe that I also know how it could be done well.

Although this answer might sound a bit risky, it does come across as sincere. Sometimes you have to take a risk to capture the decision-makers' attention. However, you also need to be prepared to be asked as a follow-up, "Okay, so how should the job not be done?" Sometimes a measured risk can pay off. Consider Wanda's experience.

### Wanda Kass—On Risk Taking

*I'm an elementary school assistant principal in a large city school system. I've been an assistant principal for four years and was a classroom teacher for seven years. It takes me 45 minutes each way to commute from the suburbs on a good day without heavy traffic. Ninety-five percent of my students are on free- or reduced-lunch. My job is very demanding; however, it does have its rewards. It's very gratifying to see our students make academic gains.*

*The commute is killing me. I applied for an assistant principal job in an urban–suburban district which is about a 15-minute drive door-to-door from my house. I'm certainly well qualified. I was invited for a screening interview with the assistant superintendent for Human Resources. He was a well-dressed man in his early 30s. I have an acquaintance who lives in the district who told me that in order to do a job there, you should most likely reside in the district.*

*We met one-on-one in his office. Dr. Smith (let's call him that) asked me for a copy of my resume and briefly skimmed it as I responded to his question about telling about myself. As I was speaking, the door quietly opened in back of me and his secretary entered, holding several papers. She placed them in front of him and, without looking up, he motioned for me to keep talking. He signed the papers and the secretary quietly took them off the desk and left the room. I was then asked what I knew about the district, and his phone rang. He held his hand up, signaling for me to stop, while he made plans on where to meet the caller for lunch. Dr. Smith mumbled, "Sorry about that," and I continued where I had left off. I had been in his office for less than 10 minutes and was answering a question about how I would introduce myself to the faculty when he slowly got up and retrieved a Manila folder from atop a nearby table.*

*I stopped talking. Dr. Smith froze for a moment and looked directly at me for the first time since we had said hello. I said, "Dr. Smith, it seems that you have no interest in me. I want you to know that I took a personal day off and left my students in order to make this appointment. I'm a highly qualified and serious candidate." There were several other things that I thought of saying, but I decided in the moment to filter myself. I wanted to be professional.*

*To my surprise, Dr. Smith smiled and said, "I like your spunk. I want you to meet the superintendent. Ten minutes later I was meeting with the superintendent. She must have liked me because I did interview with the board. No, I did not get that job. However, six months later I saw an ad for an assistant principal's position in the same school. I felt that I had nothing to lose, so I applied. To my delight, I was contacted and told that because they already knew me, I would skip the screening interview. Several weeks later, I interviewed with the board again. The moment I walked into the room for the interview, the board president said, "We remember you from last time. We're happy to see you again."*

*Well, I got the job! My lessons were that persistence pays off, and that if all seems to be a lost cause, it is okay to show some spunk and take a risk, as long as you remain a professional.*

### Who Is Seated Around the Table?

Be prepared to encounter an interview in which seven or more interviewers are around the table. It is important to grasp which stakeholders they might be representing. Usually, participants introduce themselves and will tell you, "Jane Smith, President of the PTA," for example. If the roles are not evident and they seem friendly, it is okay to ask, "And what is your role?"

I suggest that you quickly sketch the shape of the table on the manila folder that you carry with you. As the panelists introduce themselves, jot down their stakeholder groups. Their groups are more important to your success at this time than their names. As panelists take their turns asking their questions, you can glance at your notes. Knowing their roles will give you a much better context for the implication of the question.

For example, Mr. Smith asks, "If we asked your staff about you, in terms of how respectful you are, what would they say?" You glance down and see that Mr. Smith is a school custodian. This should not surprise you. Staff members want to be assured that they will be spoken to respectfully. But now, let us assume that Mrs. Martin, who is a school board member, asks the same question. Why would she ask that question?

This actually happened to me. The board member asked me that question. I told her that I enjoyed positive working relationships with the staff, they were a competent group of people, and I was proud to be their supervisor. After the interview, I briefly chatted with the superintendent on my way out of the building and commented on that question. He revealed that Mrs. Martin had a friend who worked in my district who was critical of me. I failed to move forward in the process. Of course, I don't know if this one comment was the cause, but I did pick up on the disconnect between the role of the questioner and the question.

On another occasion, a parent who was serving on a panel asked, "Describe how you get along with the Teachers' Union." Now, I would expect that question would come from a teacher who represented the union. Having done some research into the district and knowing that bitter negotiations were ongoing, my intuition was that the parent was angry with the union and looking for an administrator who would take a tough line with the union. You can see how knowing some background and being aware of who is sitting around the table can give you a valuable edge. In this instance, I was also aware that teacher representatives were usually present on the panel and I certainly did not want to alienate them.

You must use caution and diplomacy in your answers to avoid sounding hostile to one stakeholder group in deference to another group of stakeholders who might hold an opposing view on the same issue. Of course, in reality, this balancing act is what leaders do every day.

### *Tell Us about Yourself: Making Your Sandwich*

The first and most important question asked in about 95 percent of interviews is "Tell us about yourself." Other than entering the room, shaking hands, and saying hello, this is the first opportunity you have to make that first in-person impression. I cannot overstate the importance of "hitting a home run" with your response. The purpose of this question is to get the interviewee comfortable and smoothly ease into the process. Typically, in answering this query, almost everyone recites the highlights of his or her resume. Sometimes candidates start with graduating from college and play their career forward; others start with their present job and play it backwards. The interviewers already have your resume in front of them. Imagine being an interviewer and sitting through 15 candidates reciting their resumes. It can be tiresome and painful.

Rule #1 of job seeking is to distinguish yourself from the rest of the field. So, how can you be different? My advice is that you *do not start* by reciting your resume highlights. Instead, handle this first question by "making your sandwich." Whoever said "You never bring a sandwich to a banquet" was wrong.

Many years ago, I heard a clergyman deliver a moving sermon. I asked him later how he approached writing his sermons. His answer was simple: "I tell them what I'm going to say, I say it, and then I tell them what I said!" If you were asked to describe your greatest professional qualities in three words or phrases, what would you say? That's the bottom piece of bread. Then, assume you were asked to elaborate on each characteristic, what would you say? That's the meat. Then, when you have finished elaborating, review the three qualities you just described. That's the top piece of bread. You've made and delivered your sandwich. In actuality you have composed a five-paragraph thesis statement.

The three qualities that I have personally used are my 3R's: relationships, rigor, and relevance. Reciting the three qualities is the bottom piece of bread of my sandwich. I then elaborate by providing evidence of my accomplishments that embody each of these characteristics. This is the meat. I then finish off by restating the qualities one last time—the top piece of bread. Years ago, Senator Gary Hart was a very attractive, but seemingly shallow, presidential candidate. His opponent destroyed Hart's bid by pointing out Hart's lack of substance with the quip, "So where's the beef?" The "meat" of your sandwich must be rich in substance.

If you choose to take this approach, you will need to calculate which three of your qualities match up to the role and job description. The following list of characteristics are attractive qualities in most leadership position: relationships, excellence, organization, determination, resilience, collaboration, skillfulness, creativity, frugality, coach, judgment, diligence, problem solver, go-to person, professionalism, child advocacy, entrepreneurial spirit, loyalty, compassion, reliability, and persistence. Of course, you must back up your assertions with your accomplishments.

Incidentally, one reason I chose the 3R's is that they are easy for me to remember. I recommend that in preparing for the interview, you organize and carry in a manila folder with your three descriptive words or phrases written in small letters on a corner of the folder's cover. Also bring several additional copies of your resumes in the folder, in the event that someone needs a copy. The three phrases on the folder are designed as an emergency measure in case you get nervous at the beginning of the interview and draw a blank. This should be all you will need.

To illustrate how to select and "lay down the meat," let us return to one of my 3R's—relationships. Here's my partial and abridged script.

> Working in schools is all about people and developing and building upon relationships with every member of that school community. As a school principal, I took pride in knowing the name of every student. I knew their parents and their older siblings. One of the first things that I'll do, should I get this position, is to have one-on-one conversations with every employee in the school—even if it's only ten to fifteen minutes long. I want to know what they think are the strengths and the needs of the school and their department. Every relationship starts with a conversation. The conversation is the relationship.

Most interviewees talk too much. Nothing is more tiresome in the late afternoon, after working a long day, than for interviewers to sit through a candidate droning endlessly about what is already in front of them on a resume. So, answer questions, every question, in no more than two to three minutes—three minute tops. If the panel wants to hear more, then they will ask you to elaborate. Again, this is your opportunity to make a positive first impression. I do believe that interviewers begin to form an opinion on if they like you within the first few minutes of meeting you. If they like you, they then unconsciously look for reasons to reinforce and enhance that first impression. If their initial impression is negative, you then have the challenge of digging yourself out of an abyss.

Decide on how you will answer that first question and rehearse your response numerous times in front of someone or in front of a mirror. A coach can be very helpful in assisting you in crafting your response and providing objective feedback on your prepared narrative. Time your presentation. Make your actual response as natural as possible. It should not come across as rehearsed. Lay out the bottom piece of your bread this way: "You already have my resume in front of you, so rather than running through it, let me tell you about who I am by relating what my colleagues might likely say." I finish off with the top piece of bread like this. "To briefly summarize, I'm all about relationships, rigor, and relevance. Let me briefly elaborate on each quality." If you see the panelists write down your three qualities as you summarize, then you have hit a home run. That is the importance of laying down that top piece of bread: it provides clarity and closure.

### Tell Your Story

An interview is your opportunity to define yourself: to make an impact. Storytelling is a brief but powerful strategy for effective interviewing. Every aspect of job seeking is an opportunity to tell your story. Your resume and cover letter, how you present yourself, every answer to interview questions, every conversation you have, the questions that you ask, what your references say, all contribute to your narrative. Therefore, you need to carefully think through and deliberately decide upon the picture that you will present of yourself for each job campaign. You are the product, and your story is your marketing strategy.

Good stories touch people's hearts. Hearts are touched when the story rings true, resonates with the listeners' experiences and values, and makes them feel good about your character. You are the leading actor. We all have life stories. The challenge is to use interviewers' questions as prompts to weave the fabric of an authentic relevant story. The nature of the story should be crafted so that it matches the culture and values of the school–community and simultaneously responds to the question.

In answering a question about getting kids to take their schoolwork more seriously, I might, in a blue-collar community, tell them about my father. He worked as a custodian at a New York airport. My parents always encouraged me to be an excellent student, go to college, and work with my head and not with my back. This story is true. It resonates with the listeners because this represents their own dreams as parents and teachers for their children. Because of my parents' encouragement, I took my studies seriously and fulfilled my parents' dreams. This touches the panelists' hearts and makes them feel like they know who I am.

In an affluent community, I might be asked about my experience with encouraging art and music. I would emphasize my own interest in the arts, and the value of my son's high school experiences as a vocalist and what that has meant to him throughout his life. A story is effective when it is personal. I regularly go to the New York Broadway theater. The Berkshires is one of my favorite vacation spots, where I attend Jacob's Pillow for modern dance performances. Rather than simply declaring I am committed to the arts, I have, by sharing my personal activities, made clear my heartfelt commitment.

As an interviewer, I remember how impressed I was with a candidate who told us about what she did to become a more proficient Spanish speaker when she was working in an urban school where 90 percent of the students spoke Spanish at home. I also vividly recall a candidate who extensively traveled throughout Africa and lived in a small village as a Peace Corps worker. Although these folks were not necessarily the most qualified, they were among the most interesting and memorable candidates, and the best match for our large non-English speaking community.

One of the most memorable interviewees I encountered was asked, "When did you decide you wanted to be a teacher?" She replied, "When I was a little girl, maybe five or six years old, when I got home from school and finished my milk and cookies, I would go into my room and line up my dolls as if they were my students in my classroom. I would teach them everything that I learned that day in school." Such stories are not told to be manipulative, but they resound with authenticity and sincerity. These stories touch our hearts, and we want these people to work with our children because they are special.

We appreciate a good personal story told by a good storyteller. Consider how this worked out for Thomas Lewis.

### Thomas Lewis—On Telling His Story

*I am a seven-year veteran middle school math teacher who had recently obtained my administrative certification. My school district was having a budget crisis and was laying off scores of teachers including me. I've been told that what's apparent when you meet me is that I'm animated, energetic, fast talking, likeable, and bright. I had interviewed three times for assistant principal positions. All of these screening interviews resulted from personal contacts within those districts. In each case, I didn't advance to the next step. The feedback I received was that the interviewers liked me, but I did not have enough experience. I assumed my internship experiences were pretty typical. I had checked on book orders, assisted in cafeteria and bus duties, sat in on some interviews for substitute teachers—all routine duties. This isn't much to work into a resume and cover letter in order to attract attention. How could I distinguish himself?*

*However, there is more to my story that had been left untold. I grew up around boating. At the age of 15, I was teaching the art of sailing. By 18, I was supervising and training 10 sailing instructors, and two years later I was running the sailing school. I revised my* resume and prominently placed these "Other Experiences" directly under my "Professional Experiences." A friend jokingly called these revisions "resume feng shui"!

I'm the oldest of seven children. As we can imagine, in large families, the older children are expected to take on a good deal of responsibility in the home, including looking after and serving as a role model for younger siblings. Older children of large families take on a leadership role; they mentor their brothers and sisters. And so, although somewhat of an unorthodox tactic, I wrote in the second paragraph of my new cover letter about being the oldest of seven and that I grew up as "a natural-born leader." I elaborated that as a student-athlete, I was always selected as team captain, and how I was an unofficial teacher leader. It worked. The newly tailored resume and cover letter resonated, and I got interviews. When an interviewer asked me to tell about myself, I told them about the sailing school and being the oldest child. My story reveals someone who would be comfortable in a leadership role. Given my positive personal qualities and my potential as a leader, within weeks, I had two job offers.

### *Guiding Principles*

One of the most important pieces of advice I can give candidates is to "define yourself professionally by speaking to your guiding principles." Guiding principles are the beliefs and values that comprise the fabric of who you are professionally and of what you are unwilling to compromise. These principles guide your decision making and your practices.

When responding to a question in an interview, be guided implicitly by your principles. Do not say, "Whenever I need to discipline a student I am guided by my principle of 'Do No Harm.'" Instead, say, "I would need to be extremely thorough in my investigation because it would be unacceptable and unjust to accuse an innocent child of wrongdoing."

Your answer to many questions should be rooted in a guiding principle. The artistry of interviewing is your ability to effortlessly craft your response by integrating your guiding principle into the basis of your answers. The artistry comes into play when you apply a guiding principle while sounding like a practical person who speaks plainly.

I suggest you think through your guiding principles. Write them down. Once you are satisfied that you have identified the most important ones, then consider how you will use them in crafting your answers to interview questions. The integration of principle and practice is not easy, but it can be most impressive. Here are my GUIDING PRINCIPLES:

1. **Guiding Principles**—The first guiding principle is that professionals must have guiding principles. They are the beliefs and values that are the

fabric of who we are professionally and what we are unwilling to compromise. These principles are practical because they guide our decision making and professional practices.

2. **Purpose**—Our professional purpose is that we are all about student learning. Student learning should not be confused with student performance measured by achievement tests.

3. **Do No Harm**—Never physically, emotionally, or psychologically hurt anyone, or tolerate anyone one else doing harm. Safety is primary and is a precursor to learning.

4. **Build Constituency**—If you want your constituents to like and respect you, you've got to like and respect them first. We cannot function without the support of our constituencies (students, parents, teachers, supervisors, community). Relationships are key; they are the secret sauce.

5. **Be a Presence**—There is a difference between being visible and being a presence. Being a presence means interacting with constituents, not just being there.

6. **Staff Development**—Healthy schools stimulate professional growth and continuously improve our collective professional practice. It comes in many forms; the least effective are courses and presentations. The most effective approaches are coaching, peer coaching, collegial circles, action research, and case studies.

7. **Supervision and Evaluation**—The process of supervising and assessing the extent to which an objective is being fulfilled should be based upon data and evidence. *Data is a means to measure what a learner knows and is able to do.* Using data to better inform instruction will improve learning. *Feedback is an essential part of the learning process.*

8. **Every learner is unique, and we must inclusively teach the whole child.** Including and accommodating students by embracing the belief that the "least restrictive environment" enhances learning for all students and prepares them for the "real world." Likewise, celebrating cultural diversity and advocating for equity will improve learning for all.

9. **Reading, writing, speaking, and listening across the content areas are essential for higher achievement.** This should include the selection of a variety of appropriate literature and materials, including nonfiction, and assigning differentiated projects designed to engage all students.

10. **Teaching for Understanding**—Demonstrations of students' understanding of concepts or skills include the student actively: explaining, generalizing, transferring knowledge, applying skills and knowledge,

providing evidence and examples, and analogizing or creating a metaphor. *Three things, and only three things can be taught: knowledge, skills, and attitudes.* However, you can't teach what you don't know. Notice how Alexis Cardenas did not use her guiding principles:

## *Alexis Cardenas—On Guiding Principles*

*I'm an elementary school assistant principal and I've been seeking to move up to a principalship. I'm pretty well positioned because most elementary schools are fairly small, less than five hundred students, which does not warrant a second administrator. So, there are few elementary assistant principals around, making me quite competitive. Before moving into administration, my primary focus was on student learning. I was an active participant on school and district committees which dealt with curriculum, instruction, and staff development. Now, as an assistant principal, I spend most of my time in dealing with student discipline referrals, supervising buses during arrival and dismissal, doing cafeteria duty, and organizing student achievement testing programs. In between all of these administrative functions, I try to get into classrooms by doing walk throughs and doing teacher observations and writing observation reports. I'm assigned to observe about 30 percent of our teachers.*

*Thus far in my job search I've applied to about twelve jobs, have gotten nine interviews, moved onto a second or third round of interviews seven times, and have been a finalist one time in which I met with the board. They asked me about, among other questions, what qualities I would look for in hiring a new teacher, and what I "brought to the table" that would make me an outstanding principal. I felt satisfied with my responses to their questions. Needless to say, I was disappointed to find out that I didn't get the job. The superintendent personally called me to give me the news. I asked her for feedback. Her response jolted me. How could I have dropped the ball so badly? She told me, "You never even once mentioned students, learning, and teaching for understanding." She continued, "Your answers were all focused on curriculum development, accountability, and assessment results. They wanted to hear about what you would do for kids and learning."*

*I had forgotten about my own "guiding principles"; namely, it's all about student learning, and maintaining rigorous expectations for all students. What a wakeup call! You can't get so caught up in the day-to-day administration of the school and lose sight of what schools are really all about—it's all about the kids and their learning. I'll never forget this lesson.*

## **The Interviewing Process**

Now you have had a 20-minute screening interview. Your resume and cover letter did what they were designed to do—get you an interview. What is next?

Most hiring processes have four steps: the screening interview, a committee interview, a small group interview with some Central Office administrators, and an interview with the superintendent which may include the board. The nature of each step is unique, calling for different strategies. At each step, you will need to adjust your approach depending upon the duration of the interview, the cast of characters you will meet, the kind of questions that will be asked, the questions that you might ask, and the priorities of the interviewers.

*Screening interviews* typically run 10–15 minutes. Typically, three people will be interviewing about twenty candidates. Often, they are done virtually. For an assistant principal position, expect that you will meet the assistant superintendent for human resources, the principal, and an assistant principal. Their goal is to form an impression of you. They will probably ask you to tell them about yourself. They may also ask, "What do you know about us?"; "Why do you want to work here?"; or "Why do you want to be a leader?" They will have time for only about four or five questions.

The *committee interview* team may vary in size from 6 to 10, depending on the time of year. After school closes, fewer teachers and parents are available. The committee will probably speak to 8–12 candidates for about 20–30 minutes each. Be prepared to wait because it is difficult for a large group to stay on time. These interviews are usually in person. Often, the committee will receive a list of suggested questions, and each member will be asked to choose a question. The senior interviewers will go last. Expect that they might "turn up the heat" by getting specific, following up on your previous answers, and picking over your resume. You should also be prepared to solve an open-ended scenario or even role-play how you would deal with a challenging interaction.

If you make it to the next step, the number of candidates will be down to three or four. Expect to meet with *Central Office* people for about thirty minutes. They will pick apart your resume and challenge your judgment: "Why did you leave […]?" "How would you deal with a veteran teacher who is not responsive to your suggestions?" "What if you disagree with your supervisor's decision?"

The final step may be with the *superintendent* or even the Board of Education. Do not be surprised if the superintendent does more of the talking. She or he may want to give you some background and share some of the special problems you will be facing. Expect that you will then be asked how you would deal with these problems. Be prepared at this point to ask your questions.

Even the questions you ask will add layers to your story. Ask about the kinds of professional development opportunities that are available to school leaders. Find out if the district will provide you with a mentor. Inquire about the kind of expectations district leaders will have for you in your first year. These questions help paint a more vivid picture of a professional who wants to continue to grow, learn, and wants to please.

Each step in the process has its own inherent challenges. You have to be prepared to make strategic adjustments. I cannot overemphasize the importance of having a good coach along the way to help you strategize and make those adjustments. As any experienced football or basketball coach will tell you, do not expect that what works in the first quarter will necessarily work in the next quarter.

### High-Impact Questions

*How Do You Supervise?*

An often-used question for aspiring leaders is "How would you supervise a veteran teacher who is not responsive to feedback?" This question is designed to probe your knowledge of supervision, your judgment, and your interpersonal intelligence. What are some of the "guiding principles" that will control your thoughtful response?

I suggest that the main guiding principle for supervision is that of stimulating professional growth and development, and that depends on getting the teacher to self-reflect. The supervisor's job is to help the teacher, and not to bully or threaten the teacher. Anyone who feels threatened or criticized goes into a defensive mode.

Defensiveness can take on a variety of forms. Here are a few examples:

1. Some teachers just give you *lip service*, agreeing with everything you say, and then continue to do what they have been doing all along. This is designed to get you off their backs.
2. Some *take the offensive*. I have seen cases in which the teacher has more years of classroom experience than the supervisor. The veteran teacher may actually say, "I've been teaching here for 20 years, and no one has ever criticized my teaching. How long were you in the classroom?"
3. Another example is the veteran *playing the victim*. One supervisor was approached by the union president who told him that the teacher was being harassed and was so stressed that he had to go to the doctor to be treated for stress. The unspoken message from the union is "Back off. You're wasting your time trying to change veteran teachers. Spend your time supervising the non-tenured teachers."

The supervisor's job is to supervise all teachers by supervising to the evidence. That means to gather data and evidence and accurately reflect that back to the teacher without making judgments. Reflecting evidence is like holding up a mirror to help the teacher look at himself or herself. Then the supervisor facilitates a reflective conversation: "How do you interpret this evidence?" "If you had the opportunity to change the lesson, what changes would you make?" "How would you know if the revised lesson was more effective?" "What evidence or data would you collect?" The only one who can change the teacher's practices is the teacher.

In working with the veteran teacher who is not responsive to feedback, I have had success meeting the individual where he or she was, using his or her personal interests, and supporting his or her work. Over time, a sense of appreciation and trust builds. Once I have some capital, meaning credibility and trust with the person, he or she will be more open to feedback.

## *The Difficult Staffer*

Every school–community has difficult and resistant people. They come in several varieties. Here are a few notes of caution and a little dose of advice on how to deal with these folks. Let's first make a few assumptions about these folks:

1. Almost all teachers come to work every day and in their own minds bring their A game. If that "game" does not measure up to professional standards, then treat the deficit as a professional development opportunity.
2. Supervisors should never be sucked into looking and acting like bullies by behaving as if these are win–lose situations.
3. The faculty is made up of intelligent people who recognize naysayers for what they are. Most rank-in-file teachers do not want to get involved with petty school politics and personalities; they just want to do their jobs.
4. If you give negative situations more energy than they deserve, you will be "fertilizing weeds" which will then be more likely grow. Do not squander your energies in unproductive ways.
5. It is best to deal with potential problems and conflicts privately.
6. We should always supervise to the evidence and data. Leaders should gather data and artifacts as they relate to teaching and learning and compliance with procedures and policy.
7. If there is evidence that someone is under-performing, we should always deal with the problem as an opportunity for staff development and supervision.
8. We all learn best and change our behaviors as a result of reflecting on our own practices and deciding that we need to make corrective actions. In short, the supervisor is the professional, a role model who never acts like a bully.

## Responding to Unanticipated Questions

You will encounter unanticipated interview questions from time to time. The more experience you have in interviewing and/or being coached, the fewer surprises there will be. When you get a question that you have not thought through, buy a little time to think. Pause—everyone admires thoughtful people. You might even say, "Let me think about that for a second." You can also use the props in front of you. If interviewers provide water, open the bottle, pour it if they have a cup, and take a sip—and then answer. Buy time. Something will come to you.

## Answering the Union's Questions

Most committees have union representatives at the table. The union has an interest in seeing that any new supervisor will be sensitive, and perhaps even friendly, to union members. Union representatives do not want candidates who might be hard on teachers, unreasonable, insensitive to teachers' needs, or ignorant of contractual obligations and the right to due process. Of course, administrators are also on the committee, and they are listening carefully to your answers to make sure that you will be a loyal member of the administrative team. You clearly have to walk a fine line.

How do you handle questions from union reps without alienating administration? Here are a few suggestions:

- Assure everyone that you will always provide full opportunities for due process and will never knowingly violate the terms of the contact.
- Indicate that you will fully and fairly investigate any allegations brought to your attention, looking at all the evidence. In other words, do your due diligence.
- Assert that you are always guided by the principle of "do no harm" to children and that if you discover that a child is being hurt, it is your duty to protect them and every child.
- Make clear that you respect teachers, will safeguard their academic freedom, and appreciate that they have a difficult job.
- Guarantee that you will protect teachers from unreasonable demands of parents.
- Be guided by the guiding principle that you will be "firm, fair, and friendly."

## *Student Discipline Scenario*

Responding to scenarios has become more of a common interview format. It targets your ability to think on your feet, the soundness of your judgment, and the guiding principles that drive your practice. This approach is effective on many levels and is quite revealing.

Here is a brief scenario that I've often used:

> Norberto, a student who is known to be a little restless but has not been a discipline problem, is brought to your office by a security guard with a note from the teacher. The note reads, "Disrespectful. I will not tolerate this behavior." The security guard doesn't know what happened.
>
> Norberto says, "I walked over to the basket to throw away a piece and paper and the teacher starts screaming at me that I'm disrespectful and she throws me out. I don't know what the problem was."
>
> The assistant principal has Norberto stay in the office and visits privately with the teacher. The teacher says, "He was at the basket off to my side and gave me the middle finger. A couple of kids laughed. I cannot tolerate this behavior. He will not return to my class until he apologizes."
>
> Be aware that this teacher regularly refers discipline problems to you— probably 25% of your total referrals come from this teacher.

Which guiding principles will determine how you will respond? My relevant guiding principles in this case are *"Do no harm" and "Do due diligence."* This means that the administrator must be just in his/her determination and must thoroughly investigate all of the details. The administrator needs to walk around the case 360 degrees, looking at it from all angles, before reaching a conclusion.

With these as my guiding principles, what would I do? I suggest that the administrator independently question several key witnesses. I would ask the teacher for the names of the students who she reported to have laughed when Norberto was at the basket. I would then ask the teacher where these students were seated, and then I would independently interview each student and ask what he or she saw.

The interviewer interrupts, "Let's say that the teacher identifies four kids, and they all sit near the basket. Three of the kids report that Norberto looked at them and made a funny face, and they laughed. The fourth witness indicates that she wasn't watching Norberto and didn't see anything and was puzzled why a few kids laughed."

I would then ask each of the remaining three students, "Did you see what Norberto did with his hands?"

The interviewer adds, "One kid doesn't know. The other two say, 'Norberto threw a piece of paper in the basket and had a pencil in his other hand.'"

Then I would ask, "Did he do anything else with his hands?"

The interviewer answers, "They both say, 'Nothing,'" and adds, "What is your conclusion?"

My response is "I'd conclude there's no evidence that Norberto flipped his finger at the teacher. I believe that the students' laughter incited the teacher, and she believed that the laughter was derisive of her."

The interviewer presses on, "What would you do as a follow-up?"

I respond, "I would briefly review my findings with the teacher and let her know that I wanted to speak to her at the end of the day. I would tell Norberto that there was a misunderstanding and then send him back to class. And then I'd call Norberto's parent and let him or her know there was a misunderstanding that Norberto had been sent to the office, that it was cleared up, that Norberto is fine and now back in class. If the parent wanted more information, then the parent could call me after school. I would then have an 'uncomfortable' conversation (uncomfortable for the teacher) with the teacher when he or she was available."

The quality and scope of your answer often determine the future of your candidacy.

### General Questions

Once you get an interview, it is all about preparation and delivery. You cannot do anything about the competition—insiders/outsiders, more experience, local people. The key variables under your control are the quality of your preparation and the effectiveness of your delivery. An important aspect of your preparation is anticipating the interviewer's questions. Fortunately, many questions are fairly predictable. Questions generally fall among 6–10 themes for entry-level positions; more for middle managers and Central Office. Here are the typical themes: (1) telling about yourself, (2) supervising the veteran teacher who may not be responsive, (3) observing and evaluating personnel, (4) using technology, (5) helping teachers who are having student discipline problems, (6) relating to your supervisor, (7) demonstrating leadership, (8) developing your staff, (9) dealing with difficult parents, and (10) inquiring about what you know about the school and district.

You will encounter other types of questions, but these themes are the main focus. The strategies you take in responding are crucial. These are some of *the most often asked questions*:

1. Tell us about yourself. Make your resume come alive.
2. Why do you want to become a leader?
3. What do you know about our school/district? Why do you want to work here?
4. How would you deal with a veteran teacher who is not receptive to your recommendations?
5. What characteristics do you look for in an excellent teacher?
6. What do you look for when doing a teacher observation?
7. What process would you follow in doing a teacher observation and evaluation?
8. What expertise do you bring to your staff to enhance student learning through the use of technology?
9. How do you know (what evidence do you seek) that students understand the concepts and skills that are being taught?
10. How would you go about assisting a teacher who is having difficulty with classroom management and student discipline?
11. What are the most productive ways of doing staff development so that teachers can increase academic rigor and enhance their teaching repertoires?
12. Assume that your primary assigned duties are doing classroom observations; supervising buses, corridors, and cafeteria; scheduling assessments; student discipline; and ordering textbooks and other supplies and materials. How will you learn to become a more effective instructional leader?
13. How would you go about leading a committee charged with increasing academic rigor?
14. How would you deal with a fight in the corridor?
15. What kind of sessions would you choose and attend if you attended a major educational conference?
16. What would you do if you discovered that one of your teachers was referring 40 percent of the school's total student discipline cases?
17. If you were tasked with designing a new report card, how would you go about doing so?
18. What would you do if your supervisor made a decision with which you disagreed and which you felt might harm children?
19. If you interviewed candidates for a teacher vacancy, what three questions would you ask them?

20. Tell me about a student whom you helped in a way that might have changed that child's life.
21. How would you deal with a parent who is dissatisfied with how a teacher is conducting his or her class? Assume that the parent has already spoken to the teacher.

## Sample Answers to Frequently Asked Questions

Throughout various sections of this book, I provide answers to some commonly asked interview questions. More importantly, I have illustrated strategies for how to answer these questions. I have laid out a "sandwich" template on how to respond to that most important first question, "Tell us about yourself." I've provided you with *guiding principles* and illustrated the strategy of using your guiding principles in formulating answers. To assist you even more, I will now lay out a few sample answers to some of the most frequent questions:

*Q:* "Why do you want to be a school leader?"

*A:* "As a teacher, I see myself as a teacher-leader in the school, an informal leader. My reputation in the school is that I'm someone who is perceived to have good judgment, to have a moderate point of view, and to be a steady and consistent performer. I've served on many of the committees in my school, including curriculum, wellness, and school safety. I find that when I speak, people tend to listen. When I was growing up, as an athlete, my teammates looked to me to be a leader. Leaders effect change and bring about improvement. I aspire to have an ability to impact not just what happens in my classroom with my 120 students, but with what happens throughout the school with over 1,200 students. I ascribe to the principle of being professional, appropriate, sensitive and respectful."

"I bring a maturity and understanding in knowing what is appropriate. This may be a faculty meeting, department meeting, in the school corridor. I am conscious of who is speaking, what the root issue might be, and what I might have to offer. If and when I speak or act, I look around to detect any cues as to how it's being received. Before I act, I think through what I am going to say and how I am going to say it."

*Q:* "What do you know about the school district, and why do you want to work here?"

*A:* "I like being associated with excellence and that's why I want to come here and work with you. I have researched your student achievement results, and they are very good. I have spoken with several of your staff members and they told me about your initiatives in literacy, your fine special education support, the training they received when you started your International Baccalaureate program. I am aware of your athletic teams' recent accomplishments in volleyball, track and field, and basketball. I have family and friends who live here, and they are very satisfied with the high quality of education that their children receive, and the quality of colleges that your kids get into. I've also driven around to see your schools and have been impressed with the maintenance of the facilities. All this speaks well of you. I want to be part of this tradition."

*Q:* "How can the use of technology enhance teaching and learning?"

*A:* "Computers are powerful tools. However, in some cases, technology is used as an electronic page turner or workbook. I think that having a variety of instructional modalities is beneficial to students. When technology is used in its powerful forms, it can be especially advantageous. As a teacher, I like to offer a computer-based simulation of how a complex organ system works, with all of its interactions and movements. Such a strategy captures far more attention than I could achieve with a two-dimensional drawing.

I'm also a proponent of project-based learning. I believe in giving students projects to explore and freeing them to become researchers. They gather information and data and they create their own knowledge. The students should be able to create databases. They can use the technology to create reports and generate presentations. Knowledge work with technology is a wonderful approach to project-based learning."

*Q:* "How do you know, what evidence do you seek, that students are learning the concepts and skill that are being taught?"

*A:* "We shouldn't confuse student learning with how they do on teacher-made tests or scores on achievement tests. The question is, 'How do you know that students are actually learning?' To me, learning means student understanding. How do you know they understand the concepts or skills you are teaching? I know that there is understanding when I ask a question, have all students independently write out their answers, and then walk around the classroom checking answers. This approach is far superior to the teacher asking a question, students raising their hands, and then one student answering correctly. All we know, in this situation, is that the students who raised their hands thought they knew the answer, and one student demonstrated understanding. Student learning grows out of maintaining high student expectations. Demonstrations of student understanding include the student's explaining, generalizing, transferring of knowledge, applying skills and knowledge, providing evidence and examples, and creating an analogy or metaphor. That's how you know students understand. I would ask a question at the end of the lesson which gets at one of these demonstrations and have the students hand in an exit ticket at the end of class. That would give me data as to the extent of understanding."

*Q:* "What are the most productive ways of doing staff development so that teachers may enhance their teaching repertoire?"

*A:* "There are many forms of staff development. Too often, staff development is limited to presentations at after-school faculty meetings and superintendent's conference days. Too many forms of staff development are unproductive in terms of changing teachers' practices and enhancing their repertoire. The research says that presentations, workshops, and courses are about ten percent effective in changing or enhancing teacher practice. If the goal is to stimulate professional growth and development, then these approaches fail ninety percent of the participants. What other forms of staff development are more effective? Approaches such as collegial circles, peer coaching, clinical observation, and action research are all quite effective. These forms range from forty to ninety percent effective."

*Q:* "How would you continue to learn to be an even more effective instructional leader if most of your time is spent on student discipline and managing buses and lunchrooms?"

*A:* "Those responsibilities may not be glamorous, but they are essential in running the school. Somebody needs to do them, and they need to be done well. Someday I would like to become an instructional leader, and I would like to become a principal. But for now, I will do whatever the principal needs me to do, but I would appreciate any opportunity to learn more about the instructional side of things. I would like the principal and the other supervisors to act as my mentors. I'd also appreciate any available opportunities to receive state-of-the-art training."

*Q:* "How would you go about leading a committee charged with enhancing academic rigor?"

*A:* "Anytime you are involved in leading a committee, a group dynamic process takes over. The key steps in the group dynamic process are form, storm, norm, conform, and reform. What does that mean? You bring together a group of people; you 'form' a group. You get to know each other, and you clarify and define your task. Group members volunteer for different roles and assignments. You get them organized and develop a work schedule. This, too, is formation. You then generate ideas about what the curriculum is going to be, how it will be designed, and how you are going to deal with raising standards. Members are going to have different ideas, and many of these ideas may seemingly be going to be in conflict with one another. There is, figuratively, a 'storm,' a series of disagreements. The process might become quite contentious. My experience is that committees can't get from the beginning to the end without going through a storm. It is a natural part of the process. The 'norm' phase comes in when you begin to analyze what the differences are and begin to work out compromises among the seemingly disparate opinions. You work towards consensus; that's the 'conform' aspect. You find middle ground and integrate different approaches into workable approaches. Finally, you get approval and put the new 'reformed' curriculum into practice."

*Q:* "What characteristics do you look for in an excellent teacher?"

*A:* "High intelligence and knowledge in the content area are essential. You can't teach what you don't know. I also look for someone who can relate to kids, a regular person. I look for a master of the subject area who conveys a sense of enthusiasm and a willingness to give a full day's work for a full day's pay, and someone who can show me some evidence of being well organized. In a classroom setting, what overrides everything is a coherent lesson. That means that there's a thread that logically runs through the entire lesson from start to finish. I want to see evidence of student understanding. I want to know that, as an observer, I can tell that kids understand the concepts and the skills that are taught that day, and that the kids can explain, in their own words, what the concepts are and can demonstrate those skills satisfactorily. I want to see students provide their own examples."

### *How to Answer Killer Interview Questions*

I have been coaching school leaders and aspiring leaders in preparation for their interviews for 12 years. My clients frequently ask me how to answer questions with which they struggle. Here's a sampling of a few of those questions, my strategies as to how to answer, and my suggested answers:

1. **"What would your direct supervisor say about you if I called her?" (You think you might not get a positive recommendation from her/him)**

**Analysis:** You can't criticize your supervisor, and you can't say that she/ he might say something negative about you. What you can *do* is to speak to your boss; let her/him know that a reference call might be calling and ask for a positive recommendation that emphasizes the positive things that you've done. You might even consider making a list of a few of your accomplishments. Most supervisors are not out to destroy your career. Who knows, this might be seen by your boss as an opportunity for you to leave and motivate her/him to give you a positive recommendation?

**Answer:** "I think she will say that I have great relationships with our students and their parents, that I'm always well prepared, and that I'm always willing to give extra time and attention to assist my students."

2. **"If you get this position, how long do you plan on staying in it?"**

   **Analysis:** You don't know how long you'll stay or how things will work out. Your new supervisors probably don't want to go through additional transitions in the short run. However, you won't be credible if you say you'll stay for the remainder of your career. Employers seek leaders who are honest. Your answer needs to offer a reasonable rationale that supports your response.

   **Answer:** "Assuming that things will work out well, I think five to seven years would make sense. The literature says that it takes at least five years to implement and sustain structural improvements. I'm committed to see my work through to positive outcomes."

3. **"You're a certified school leader with very little leadership experience, why should we hire you over more experienced candidates?"**

   **Analysis:** Your aim is to present yourself as a self-confident, "can do" person who will grow on the job. Your selling points are your accomplishments as a teacher, your potential and willingness to embrace being mentored and molded into the culture of your new school and district, and your raw undeveloped potential and energy.

   **Answer:** "I may not be your most experienced candidate, but I can assure you that no one will be more eager to grow and learn, and work harder than I. I believe my colleagues will tell you that I'm a teacher leader who has played leading roles in some of our most important school improvements. My resume outlines some of these projects. Let me add that as a high school and college athlete I was often chosen as team captain. I've been told that I'm a 'natural born leader.'"

4. **"I see on your resume that you live more than an hour away. Is that going to be a problem?"**

   **Analysis:** Never hesitate to "shoot down" any obstacle that might diminish your value. You should provide evidence that any of their concerns have been overcome or resolved in the past. Employers want to be assured.

   **Answer:** "I take full responsibility for my attendance and timeliness. Although my present place of work is 15 miles less of a commute, my time in traffic commuting here would be about the same. It is fair to say that I'm never late and usually one of the first people to arrive. It's not a problem."

5. **"As an experienced school leader, tell us about a failure you experienced, and more importantly, what lesson did you learn from it?"**

   **Analysis:** This is similar to the often-asked question, "What is your greatest weakness?" The worst answer is, "I really can't think of one." Being humble and self-reflective are very desirable characteristics. The example you provide should be designed to resonate with the interviewers' experiences and evoke their empathy.

   **Answer:** "As an inexperienced leader years ago, I made decisions based on gut feelings. What I've learned over the years was to put more trust in evaluating the evidence and results; to slow down [...] to listen to people I trust and respect even when they have divergent opinions. I've learned what I call, 'watch the movie.' In other words, listen, suspend judgement, slow down, and decide on what is in the best interests of my students. The example that comes to mind was when I was a superintendent. I had a strong desire to initiate an International Bachelorette Program. As we debated the merits of the program, I became more inclined to start the program. However, I encountered some strong opposition from a segment in the community and from the teachers' union. My gut told me that it would be divisive, and I backed away from moving ahead. I regret not listening to my leadership team who advised me of the merits of the program for our students."

## *Are You Getting Your Fair Share of Interviews?*

Are you sending out your resume but only getting few interviews? Are you getting interviews but are not being called back? What should you do to get your fair share of interviews? What are the factors that determine your success?

*Factors to Consider:*

1. Attractiveness of the District—stereotypically, highly attractive districts or schools are usually affluent, high paying, and high achieving. They are highly selective in choosing candidates. Unless you are well qualified, meaning looking for a parallel position, a graduate from a prestigious university, hold a doctorate, and have significant accomplishments, your chances of getting an interview are slim. That is not to say that you should not apply, but your expectations should be realistic.

2. Quality of Your Resume—if you're a qualified candidate but are getting less than a 25–30 percent positive return (initial interview per resume submitted), then you probably have a resume problem. Your resume's job is to tell your story in a compelling manner and get you an interview. You should have your resume evaluated and edited by a credible and reputable coach. Educational resumes are somewhat unique, so be wary of having a well-meaning friend from the business world review it.

3. Effectiveness of Your Screening Interview—typically an average of about fifteen screening interviews are scheduled for a leadership position. Sometimes they only last 10–15 minutes. Obviously, there are a limited number of questions that can be asked and answered. The interviewers are trying to get a sense of who you are by evaluating how you present—your narrative (your story), your likeability, and how you would fit into their school–community. About six of the candidates will move on to the next round. If you get a screening interview and habitually do not move to the next step, then you need to evaluate your narrative and how you present yourself. You probably should be coached rather than trying to adjust on a trial-and-error basis.

4. Quality of Your Answers—the next step is The Committee Interview composed of around seven stakeholders (parents, teachers, administrators), which will run about twenty minutes. There is ample time for them to ask about eight questions encompassing a variety of educational practices. The committee will likely narrow the field down to about three finalists. The candidate needs to perform a precarious balancing act. She/he must satisfy the vested and oftentimes competing interests of parents who are demanding greater sensitivity to their child's needs and accountability, administrators who are seeking higher academic achievement, and teacher unions who are looking for teacher-friendly leaders. At the same time, the candidate must maintain a positive, thoughtful, sensitive, knowledgeable, and diplomatic demeanor. This demands extensive preparation

which includes becoming familiar with the strengths, needs, nature, and values of the school–community. A successful candidate must do his/her homework and be ready to present him/herself appropriately.

5. Flexibility—the final interview, usually two or three finalists, involves a 30- to 45-minute session with Central Office administrators. Again, there should be another shift in your strategy for this interview. These leaders are trying to determine who is the best equipped to fulfill their agenda, solve existing problems, and represent the proper image that will satisfy the community and particularly the Board of Education. I often use the metaphor of a tennis match. Up until this interview, the candidate's job is to "return serve" to each questioner. However, this match requires the candidate to be flexible in switching the "game" by creating a "volley"—a back and forth, a give-and-take conversation. This calls for your asking clarification as to the district's issues and priorities, offering your related experiences in response, and, as a result, building a professional rapport.

These are the major factors you should be aware of and act upon if you are going to get your fair share of interviews and successfully move forward in the process.

## Interview Questions for Superintendents

1. What do you anticipate being the most difficult types of challenges that you will face in our district?
2. Describe the process you use in communications among school board members and the superintendent.
3. How will you build and sustain an effective leadership team?
4. Describe a crisis to which you've responded and tell us the strategies you use to deal with and avoid crises.
5. How would you deal with a hostile and aggressive crowd attending a public meeting of the Board of Education? What plan might you put together in anticipation of such a meeting?
6. What process do you go through in developing a district budget?
7. What lessons have you learned in dealing with the Covid-19 epidemic and what changes would you seek to make which would improve the district as a result of these lessons learned?
8. Assume that there is a serious need to improve buildings and grounds; how would you go about doing capital improvement planning that might include a bond issue?

9. What is your approach to effectively evaluate teachers and school leaders that results in their professional growth and development?

10. Outline your entry plan once you are appointed and extending into your first hundred days on the job.

11. What qualities do you look for in hiring teaching and leadership candidates?

12. How do you go about making visits to schools? What do you look for?

13. How do you teach and mentor school leaders?

14. What functions and problems should the superintendent directly and personally take on?

15. Describe the process you use in developing annual district goals.

16. What role do you play in negotiations with various unions?

17. How do you determine when it is necessary to communicate with school legal counsel?

18. How do you handle superintendent–student disciplinary hearings?

19. How do you prefer to develop agendas for board meetings?

20. What should be the role of the board president?

21. What is your role in dealing with grievances?

22. How do you deal with conducting investigations of wrongdoing?

23. How do you prefer that the board do your superintendent evaluation?

24. Walk through the steps of developing and putting up a bond issue

25. How do you go about deciding on a snow day?

26. What is your approach to dealing with the union leaders?

27. How transparent is your approach to "transparency"?

28. How do you go about building district-wide morale?

29. Taking a long-term view, how do you go about sustaining positive change?

30. Describe your decision-making process

31. Tell us about an unpopular decision you made? What did you learn from it?

32. Tell us about innovations you brought about in the area of school security and public safety.

33. How do you develop positive relations with local police and fire officials?

34. What creative ideas do you have about maintaining a positive public image for the district?

35. How will you make yourself more accessible to your publics?

36. How will you deal with "special requests and favors" from "entitled" constituents?

37. How do you deal with disloyal school leaders who are critical of your leadership?

38. What would you do if you strongly disagreed with a decision of the board despite your best efforts to persuade?
39. How long do you expect to remain in the district?
40. What are your professional or personal guiding principles that are nonnegotiable?
41. How do you deal with free speech and student publications?
42. What is your vision of the future role of technology?
43. How do you deal with the ever-rising costs of special education?
44. What do you consider to be your three great professional accomplishments?
45. What are some of your ideas about cost savings?
46. What would your critics say about you?
47. What would your advocates say about you?
48. What would you want to accomplish five years from now that would lead us to agree that you have been a successful leader?
49. Tell us about a student, or teacher, or school leader who you feel you helped change the course of his/her life.

## What Questions Should You Ask During the Interview?

What questions you ask depends on where you are in the process. It is important to be sensitive to the needs of the people on the interviewing committees. They are busy people who have volunteered their time to serve. The time allotted for each interview allows them to stay on schedule. I have often felt like a captive when a candidate, who is allotted 15–30 minutes for an initial interview, is asked, "Do you have any questions?" This opportunity is a courtesy. It is not an open invitation to pull out a long list of questions and take over and extend the process. If you move on in the process, you will have ample time to have more questions answered.

The question you should ask at the initial interview is "What is the next step and what is your timeline?" Often the moderator will have already answered that question. It is also okay to say, "I have many questions. However, I'll hold off hoping that I'll have an opportunity to get my answers as the process progresses." This response demonstrates your sensitivity to the committee's time constraints.

At future rounds of interviews, it is important to ask questions. The questions you ask should add texture to the portrait you are painting of yourself. Demonstrate that you are a serious professional person by asking, "What kinds of professional development opportunities would be available to me? Would I be assigned a coach?" Show that you are eager to be successful by asking,

"What do you expect me to accomplish within three months, six months, and one year?"

The most successful type of follow-up interview evolves into conversation, give-and-take, and the questions you ask can serve as triggers in such a conversation. Be prepared to respond to the answers that the committee offers. Finally, be sensitive to your interviewers' body language. If there is any sign of restlessness or distractedness, then cut short your questions.

### Memorable "One-Liners"

> I want to leave you with one last thought. Whatever challenges I have taken on in my life, I have succeeded. If I am fortunate enough for you to hire me, I promise that you will never regret your decision.

Great interviews must contain powerful and memorable statements. The last thing you say before walking out the door will be remembered.

Great lyrics, great speeches, and great interviews all deliver memorable "one-liners." Here are a few of what I sometimes call "killer one-liners."

In response to the question, "Tell us about yourself," I would say, "I am about excellence. Whatever job I take on, I give it my maximum effort. *My father taught me the value of hard work.* He would tell me that if these people are good enough to pay you, then *they deserve to get a full day's work for a full day's pay.* I'm the first one on the job in the morning. *I get there when the custodian opens the school. And I'm the last to leave at night.*"

In speaking about the critical importance of establishing and maintaining relationships, I say, *"The conversation is the relationship.* You can only get to know your colleagues, your students and their parents when you take the time and have a conversation. In my first 100 days on the job, I will have a one-on-one conversation with every member of the staff member."

What would you do if a parent called you with a complaint about how a teacher was treating his or her child? My response is, "After asking if the parent had already spoken to the teacher, I would invite him or her in the see me. *Everyone wants to be heard.* The secret of effectiveness is listening, listening actively with interest and empathy. Sometimes the parents will repeat their stories. I listen to the stories again. They may even repeat the stories a third time. Still, I listen patiently. When they've finished, I say, 'I hear you. I promise that I'll look into this problem and be back to you within twenty-four hours.'"

What would you do if your supervisor made a decision with which you strongly disagree? My answer is, "I would close the door and say, 'You know that as my boss, *you are my number one constituent.* I would never publicly contradict you. However, privately, in this case, I'd like to explain to you why I think you might be making a mistake. Still, at the end of the day, I will accept and support your decision.'"

Why do you want to be a school leader? If I were a teacher who was seeking my first administrative job, I would answer, "As a middle school teacher, I teach 110 students each year. Throughout my life, I have always assumed leadership positions. I always was chosen to be captain of my sports teams, president of the clubs and organizations to which I've belonged. I have noticed that, *when I speak, people tend to listen.* As an administrator, *I would have the opportunity to leverage my influence* from the 110 students in my classes to the 1,200 students in the school."

What would you do if a teacher is having difficulty controlling students in his or her class? I would assert, *"Most teachers come to work every day believing their bringing their A game.* I would assume that the teacher is doing his or her best and is unhappy about his or her students' behavior. This teacher needs help, and it's my job to help. This teacher is not going to improve if I beat him or her up. I see situations like this as staff development opportunities."

I always suggest that, as soon as you leave your interview, you go to your car and write down all of the questions you were asked and the responses that you gave which were particularly well received. As you gain more experience in interviewing, you will develop your own repertoire of "killer one-liners."

### *Portfolio: Show or No Show*

If you are going to bring a portfolio, then put it in a professional-looking binder. The interviewers will see it and might ask to review its contents. If not, there may be an opportunity to refer to a piece in it as a response to a question. Ask if the interviewers would like to see the artifact, but do not push it on them. If such an opportunity does not arise or if they reject your offer, you will have an opportunity at the end of the interview when they ask if you have any questions. Again, inquire if they would like to see it. Personally, when I am interviewing, I find portfolios to be a distraction.

### *Writing Samples, Essays, Role-Playing*

The secretary instructs you, "Please arrive thirty minutes before your screening interview to do a writing sample. By the way, please bring a copy of a recent teacher observation report you have done with you." The writing sample is one request that might be made of you. Some districts, as part of the application process, require applicants to write essays in response to specific questions. You may also be asked to bring along observation reports that you have recently written. In other cases, you may be asked to produce and submit a five-minute video. Finally, a role-playing activity may be part of an interview as well.

Why do districts make these demands? One reason is to cull out applicants who are not serious or cannot write well. It is easy to send a letter and resume online. By contrast, writing a required essay is demanding and time consuming. Applicants who are not committed to the process will not respond, thus eliminating themselves from the pool. Writing samples, essays, and cover letters are quickly reviewed for mechanical errors, such as typos, misspellings, grammar lapses, nonstandard capitalization, faulty subject–verb agreement, inaccurate word usage, and awkward syntax. My personnel director regularly wore a path to my office with papers in hand, exclaiming, "Can you believe this! Look at the grammar! This person has two master's degrees and is illiterate!" I must say it is a little shocking that educated people cannot handle the language, and, not surprisingly, those applications go into the "C pile."

Writing samples often take on the form of writing a letter in response to a complaint or turning down a request. Again, mechanics and organization are of primary importance. An important aspect of a supervisory position is the ability to write well. Poorly crafted written correspondence is an embarrassment. The public has an expectation that educators write well, and that expectation must be fulfilled. You cannot blame a secretary for a poorly composed piece of correspondence. There are no excuses. It is the supervisor's job to review and edit all that goes out of his or her office.

Usually, when candidates reach the final phases of their candidacy, their essays and other writings are scrutinized for their substance. In response to an essay regarding "effective teaching," a candidate might identify the importance of differentiation of instruction, among other methodologies. In preparing to interview this candidate, I might highlight various words and phrases from their writings and ask related questions such as, "What aspects of the instructional process can you differentiate?" In reviewing an observational report, I would be interested in the extent to which the collected data and evidence, the conclusions, and the recommendations were coherent. I would look for clarity of writing in explicating the arguments, observations, and implications being made.

Role-playing with a candidate during an interview has become a frequent exercise. I always saved the role-playing for last. If the candidate has not measured up to previous candidates, I would skip the role-play and wrap up the interview. Role-playing requires at least five minutes of interaction, and if I am not interested in the candidate, I will not make that investment in time.

A role-play scenario should, on the surface, appear to be simple and routine. However, as with most real-life situations, it must have nuance. Typical scenarios might take the form of handling a fight between students, a suggestion that a student walkout is being planned as a protest, a charge of sexual harassment between two teachers, or a rumor that a student has a knife. As the candidate talks through the obvious first steps, the interviewer introduces new information. Role-playing can be stressful. It is designed to reveal such critical qualities as the ability to investigate and analyze a situation and de-escalate it; use judgment, resourcefulness, and creativity; and draw on and utilize resources and resource people, communication skills, and follow-up. The candidate who demonstrates these qualities often has a make or break performance.

# CHAPTER 4

# SELF REFLECTING

## Debriefing and Reflecting

Interviews are hard to earn, even though we all try our very best. You leave the interview and your every word and the interviewers' reactions—facial expressions, nods, smiles, glances to others at the table—echo and replay in your mind. What does it all mean? Did they like me? Why didn't they like me? Did I blow the interview because of the way I answered that one question?

How do I constructively and objectively reflect on my performance? Here are a few criteria against which you might judge for yourself, remembering that we evaluate based on the evidence. So, what is the evidence that:

- They liked me,
- I distinguished myself through my introduction,
- I understood the questions and answered them appropriately,
- I demonstrated that I knew their school culture and that I was a good fit,
- I showed the maturity and the gravitas to gain respect, and
- I demonstrated good judgment.

Unfortunately, you may not be objective in your reflection. That is why you should consider working with a knowledgeable mentor or coach. Another piece of advice: do not be too self-critical. Too many interview processes are "inside jobs." You are only there for "window dressing." Many interviews and questions can be idiosyncratic. That is, the question uniquely pertains to one individual or to one local or personal event. This unpredictability does not mean that you should turn down an interview because you never know what can happen. One last thought: some places are so toxic that you simply would not want to work there.

Nepotism and xenophobia have always existed in our schools. It goes beyond just knowing someone on the inside to get a job. Sometimes you must *be* someone on the inside. I went through my schooling in the 1950s. I have visited hundreds of schools over the years and too many of them seem like a trip back into the Twilight Zone of the 1960s. This is a sad statement on the state of education, and I have come to realize that, even if asked, I would not want to work in these places. They are closed and fearful of outside people as well as outside ideas and practices. It is an educational tragedy that needs to be addressed.

Organizations that practice nepotism are resistant to change and do not honor diverse perspectives. They see only one way of doing things and are not open to new ideas even if the new approaches are better than what they are used to. Conventional wisdom seems to be that the only way to land a job in many school districts is to know someone on the inside. Sadly, at times, that assessment is accurate. It makes me wonder why are these organizations so afraid of outsiders who offer diversity of thought and perspective. I believe it is time for school organizations to collectively change their way of thinking and be more open to diversity, to encourage innovations, and to promote continued growth.

Nepotism comes in many forms. Let us limit this discussion to advantages in seeking leadership jobs. Besides being unfair, nepotism often results in mediocrity in that the best qualified candidates are passed up, and the same old practices are perpetuated, as the torch is passed to another insider who was weaned in a closed system. There is a terrible lack of "fresh air." The justification for rejecting outside candidates is often that "they're not a good fit"— which ironically is often true! Unfortunately, sometimes "outsiders" are chosen and then not listened to, sometimes even shunned. However, schools are organisms that must continue to grow and learn. The conditions for organic growth are oxygen and light. Nepotism, by contrast, thrives in dark and airless school–communities.

## How Not to Mess Up Your Interview

- **Answer the question that's been asked**. Stick to the interviewers' questions. Stay on topic. Panelists will generally ask the same questions of every candidate to compare answers. Too often candidates will "get on a roll" and go off on tangents, thereby not answering the question. Not answering the question will certainly be noticed.
- **Never fake an answer**. If you are asked about something you do not know, simply admit that you do not know it. Nobody likes a faker. You

should add, "I don't know the answer to that, but I am a quick learner and will learn whatever I need to know in order to get the job done."

- **Maintain an even keel**. Laughing too long and too loud at a joke that is not that funny, becoming overly enthusiastic about one of your own answers, and/or being argumentative and emphatic about a minor issue are all examples of "overdoing it." Professionals maintain an even keel. Act like an adult. Being over the top just raises eyebrows and generates side glances.

- **Play to the whole table**. In a group interview, you have to please everyone who is sitting around the table. You cannot afford to please administrators at the cost of alienating the teachers. Seek out the middle ground and demonstrate your diplomatic skills. Nevertheless, you should still remain true to your principles.

- **Always speak the truth**. Today, with the availability of Google, Facebook, and online newspapers, it is relatively easy to check facts. Stretching the truth and being found out is fatal. The regional educational community is a small circle. You *will* be checked out.

- **Stay calm**. Do not expect every answer to be a home run. Try not to get rattled if your answer to a question is weak. As the song says, "Just keep on keepin' on!" Interviewers are people, too. They know you are nervous, and they can be forgiving. They will recognize it if you redeem yourself.

- **Act like a guest**. I have witnessed candidates come into the room and move their table and chair to be closer to the panel. I have encountered several candidates who became insistent about setting up a PowerPoint presentation, even after being told not to do so. Most commonly, candidates can drone on and on despite being told, "Thank you. Now, let's go on to the next question." Act like a guest. You are not throwing the party.

- **Be respectful**. No matter how disrespected you might feel, always remain respectful. As a candidate, I have sat out in a waiting room for up to 90 minutes. I have been asked to do a writing sample, even though I have been published dozens of times. A questioner has criticized my current employer. Through it all, hold your tongue, smile, and be polite.

- **Leave your baggage home**. Question: "What do you expect from us in order for you to be successful?" The best response would be, "I work best as a member of a mutually supportive team." Unfortunately, I have heard candidates say, "My last boss was verbally abusive. I could not work under those conditions." Another response was, "I just want you to know that, as a parent, I have to be home by 4:30, and that I can't work nights."

The best advice that anyone can give you is to *just be yourself.* Let the interviewers know who you are and what you stand for. Be appropriate and speak from the heart.

## The Reference Check

The reference check comes at the end of the process, usually once the district leaders have settled on the last candidate but prior to making you an offer. Oftentimes, they will contact people that you might not have listed as references. If administrators have contacts in your district, they might call them, assuming they will obtain more candid opinions from someone they know. The assumption is that the references you have chosen will only say good things about you. If they get negative comments, you are probably in trouble. However, the seriousness of the quandary depends on the source and nature of the criticism. Be aware that the local teachers' union has its own network and will call around and check you out. In addition, the district's personnel administrator often contacts sources in your current district who are not on your list of references to obtain more objective opinions.

Of course, the last step is the approval of the Board of Education. Board members may have their own contacts as well—sometimes local residents who live in your district. Finally, districts will Google you and check your Facebook postings. Be careful about what is on social media about you. In particular, delete photos of inappropriate activities or dress.

### *Your References Can Be Weaponized*

You are a finalist—down to two or three candidates. How can you distinguish yourself to become the most attractive contender? You've been asked to provide a short list of references. This is what you can do beyond prepping for the last interview.

- Find out as much as you can about your competitors. Which of their experiences are and/or are not a good fit for the position? Are there gaps or weaknesses in their skill sets? Are the nature and the culture of their workplaces a good match for this school–community?
- Contact your references and prepare them for the reference call. Ask that they emphasize your experiences, skills, and knowledge that are superior and/or competitive with those of your competitors.

- Send a follow-up email or text message to your references providing each of them with a short list of qualities and descriptions of experiences that you'd like for them to speak to.
- Try to have each reference speak to different aspects of your strengths or express them in different words and phrases so, as a composite, they describe a positive, coherent and vivid picture of you.
- Never ask your references to lie or falsify any information about yourself.
- Ask them to contact you asap after their calls and review the conversation.
- During your final interview, emphasize the same assets that your references have or will have said about you.

## CHAPTER 5

# THE END GAME

### Closing the Deal

Let's count them. You have successfully undergone a paper screening, a screening interview, the hiring committee interview, and an interview with Central Office administrators. The district is now down to two or three finalists, and you will meet with the superintendent and perhaps the school board. How will those interviews be different? If you are the last person standing, how do you close the deal?

Going one-on-one with the superintendent will be a different experience from your other interviews. It may be the longest interview, probably about thirty minutes. This interaction should turn into a conversation. The superintendent will probably do most of the talking, informing you about the position. He or she will not allow you to give long answers; you'll be cut off once he or she is satisfied that the question has been answered. The interview will be quick-paced, and much ground will be covered in a short time. Expect to be challenged about your resume. "Why did you leave Happy Hollow after only three years?" "I see that you were working at ABC Corporation for a year before you started working at your position. What happened?" "If I called the Happy Hollow Superintendent, what would she say was the reason you left?" "What steps would you take in working with our math teachers to develop a curriculum that is aligned with the State standards?" "What would you do within your first 100 days on the job; in other words, what's your entry plan?" High-pressure interviews are designed to assess your composure under stressful conditions.

The superintendent might share some of the problems you might be facing. "Happy Hollow Middle School has its share of veteran teachers who can be quite resistant to responding to your recommendations. The school also has some tough union leaders. How would you deal with this?" Keep your response positive and do not reveal any misgivings.

Your reaction might be "I'm familiar with the dynamics of resistant teachers and union militancy where I've worked. This doesn't scare me. I have seen close up how my administrators successfully dealt with those challenges."

Be prepared now to ask your questions. The following is a short list of appropriate questions you might ask, if they have not been previously addressed.

- What are your expectations for my success?
- What transitional activities will be provided to assist me?
- What professional development opportunities will be available to me?
- What obstacles might I encounter? Are there any "third rails"?
- What support systems and resources are in place for me (clerical assistance, technology, office space, equipment and supplies, a mentor, special training)?
- What will be my work schedule?
- What are the next steps and timeline in this process?

Do *not* bring up the issues of salaries and benefits. These issues will be discussed when an offer is made.

If the superintendent patiently gives you detailed answers to your questions, this is a positive sign. If the superintendent mentions salary, this is a very positive indication of interest. If you are invited back to meet with the board, you should ask, "How many candidates do you anticipate the Board will meet?" The possibilities are only one, two, or three. Sometimes, the superintendent will not have you meet the board. He or she will recommend the final candidate to the board for appointment. Do not be disappointed if the superintendent is noncommittal and informs you that a couple of candidates remain to be seen and the district will get back to you. This probably means that they still need time to do a reference check.

Alert your references that they might be getting a call. Never list someone as a reference unless you are certain he or she will say only good things about you. Instruct your references to immediately let you know if they have been contacted. If your references are not called, there is a chance you might not be advancing in the process. You should also know that people in your current district who are not on your list of references might also be called.

The superintendent or the Human Resources Administrator will probably call you if you are not going to interview with the board. Unsuccessful inside candidates are usually contacted for a face-to-face meeting.

If you are the chosen candidate, you will be asked, "If you're offered the position and we can agree on salary, are you prepared to accept?" Before you talk money, you need to research where you would fall on their administrators' salary schedule. You may be asked how much you are presently making. Tell the interviewer what you will be making next year, including any additional stipends for extra assignments. You should not be expected to take a pay cut.

It is permissible to negotiate, but you need to do so professionally. This will be your only chance to negotiate. Once they make an offer, you can say, "I was hoping for something a little better. Is there any flexibility?" Asking that question can get you an extra salary step. However, if the salary is satisfactory, just smile and say, "Thank you. We have a deal."

However, the deal is *not* done yet. *Only* the Board of Education can hire someone, through a majority vote based on the superintendent's recommendation. From time to time, the board might not approve the superintendent's recommendation. This rejection is probably unrelated to the candidate and, most likely, has much to do with local politics. The reason that "runner-up" candidates do not hear back from the district during this final decision-making phase is to provide a backup in case the chosen candidate's appointment falls through. Qualified candidates will still be in line, waiting to be contacted. The district will not have to restart a new and lengthy search process. Therefore, if you are a finalist and have not had your references checked, there still might be hope. Sometimes, the "bridesmaid" gets lucky!

Let's see how Hyman Roth closed the deal after a couple of "bridesmaid" encounters.

### Harry Roth—Closing the Deal

*I've worked as a science teacher and then as a science coordinator for 16 years. I had spent my career working in small rural schools. The largest district I'd worked in had a total K-12 population of 1,100 students. Needless to say, rural districts don't pay well. They just don't have the economic base. However, there are many other benefits in working in small communities, including the feeling of being an intimate part of the life of the community.*

*Sadly, my wife was unfamiliar with and unhappy with rural life and our limited lifestyle. We separated and then divorced. We do not have any children. I was lonely. I felt trapped in my career and that my professional growth was limited. I had not experienced a more worldly life. I got a job as a science teacher for a Department of Defense Dependent school in Germany for that next school year; and there I was living and traveling in Europe. What an incredible experience for someone who had never traveled more than hundred miles away from home.*

*However, I did miss America. After a year, I returned. However, small town living and working for a meager salary no longer worked for me. I had learned to adapt to other cultures. I needed to be stimulated and grow. So, I began applying for supervisory positions in suburban areas. To my surprise, I got interviews and moved on to final rounds. I was an experienced supervisor with an interesting background. However, when I reached the final round with a superintendent, I just couldn't close the deal. The interviewing strategies that I used throughout the process didn't seem to be effective at this level. I needed help. I called a former superintendent with whom I had worked years ago. He had a diverse set of experiences, having worked in urban, suburban, and rural communities.*

*He advised me that going one-on-one with a superintendent needed to take on the form of a conversation. Answering questions from members of a panel called for a different set of strategies. He told me that superintendents are looking for a candidate who understands the challenges and problems that confront their district. Superintendents need to be assured that you have the know-how to be an asset in solving their problems and fulfilling their goals. "Get the Superintendent to do more of the talking. Ask questions of him or her which will clarify what his or her needs are. Talk about your accomplishments and experiences that relate to the district's needs and aspirations. Be an active listener."*

*His advice worked. I pictured myself as Chris Wallace asking open-ended questions and got the superintendent to open up. From time to time, I would slide a comment into the conversation about my experience which resonated with his situation. He would respond, "Yes, that's what I'm talking about. That's what we have to do." I was closing the deal.*

*As the interview began to move toward the end, the superintendent told me that he wanted me to meet with the Human Resources person. That meant we were going to talk salary. My mentor had advised me that this would be my only opportunity to ever negotiate salary. I had checked the administrators' salaries on the net and had determined the range of salaries currently being paid to their coordinators. If they offered me a salary within their range, I would accept it. If it were below or at the very bottom of the range, I was prepared to say, "Given the fact that I've served as a coordinator for five years, I'm a little disappointed with the offer. I'm not rejecting your offer, but I am hoping that you might be a little more flexible." As it worked out, I did not have to negotiate. The salary offer was fair.*

*I withheld making any announcements of my pending new job until the actual approval of the board. I was approved. I had closed the deal, and now have a wonderful future career and lifestyle ahead of me.*

Take a lesson from Harry. If you learned from his story, then you'll hear the words, "Congratulations, you're hired."

### *Your Entry Plan*

Be prepared to be asked, "If you were asked to create an entry plan, including your first 100 days on the job, what would you include?" My advice, in anticipation of being asked, is to actually create your written entry plan. If asked the question, take it out and indicate, "In anticipation to this interview, I prepared a draft entry plan for you. If you're interested, I can pass it around the table." The interviewers will be very impressed with your diligence, foresight, and preparation. Make sure to title your plan "Happy Hollow Entry Plan" and put your name on the cover page.

For the purpose of your interview, I recommend keeping the format of the plan simple. You do not need a timeline, subheadings, or graphics. The following is a list of suggestions for the position of assistant principal:

- Meet with the principal to come to a common understanding about his or her expectations for me.
- Arrange for a tour of the building by the head custodian.
- Arrange with the school union representative to go from room to room on the "first day back for teachers" to say hello.
- Arrange with the PTA president for a driving tour of the district.
- Ride a school bus route.
- Obtain copies of various plans, studies, and important documents such as union contracts, student code of conduct, professional performance plan, staff development plan, technology plan, fire drill procedures, school safety plan, school budget and codes, capital improvement plan, master schedule, and Board of Education policies.
- Review important school data such as assessment scores, attendance reports, and disciplinary reports.
- Meet with other school administrators and supervisors to better understand their roles, the school structures, and current initiatives and concerns.
- Obtain a copy of a recent yearbook with photographs of staff members.
- Meet with the student council.
- Meet with the PTA.
- Join the regional assistant principals' association.
- Meet with the local members of the administrators' association.
- Meet one-on-one with every member of the certified staff for 10–15 minutes about their views about the school's strengths and needs.
- Attend Board of Education Meetings, PTA meetings, Athletic and Music Boosters, and Special Education Advisory Council Meetings.
- Create a database of staff birthdays.
- Join the local Chamber of Commerce.

- Develop a report on what you have learned as a result of completing the 100-Day Plan and discuss it with the principal.

## *Being Interviewed by a Board of Education*

Over the last several years boards of education have become more actively involved in interviewing and selecting candidates for leadership positions. State law dictates that only the board can make personnel appointments. Of course, board members are elected officials and as such they have their own priorities and can be influenced by their constituents. Consequently, if a candidate is going to be interviewed by the board, you need to find out who they are and what their priorities might be.

Find out the occupation of board members. The kind of questions that a professional educator might ask are different from those of an accountant, or a teacher, or a real estate agent. Does the trustee have a child in the special education program, or is he or she involved in youth athletics, the music boosters, or the performing arts? Board members for the most part are parents and will ask the kind of questions that parents ask. Be prepared to answer questions like these:

1. What expertise do you bring to your staff in enhancing student learning through the use of technology?
2. How would you go about assisting a teacher who is having difficulty with classroom management/student discipline?
3. How would you go about determining what your priorities should be in your new position?
4. How would you deal with a veteran teacher who is not receptive to your recommendations?
5. What characteristics do you look for in an excellent teacher?
6. What would you do if your supervisor made a decision that you disagreed with and you felt would harm children?
7. How would you deal with a parent who is dissatisfied with how a teacher is conducting his/her class? Assume that the parent has already spoken to the teacher.
8. If you interviewed candidates for a teacher vacancy, what three questions would you ask them?
9. What would you do to attract more students into the music and arts programs?
10. What would you do to support the philosophy of inclusion in our special education program?

Beware that some board members can be aggressive and/or argumentative in how they ask questions and may challenge you. Do not fight back. Keep your cool, remain professional, and if you don't agree, just say: "That's an interesting point. I will have to think about that."

A final reminder. Remember that the two most important factors in getting a job are being likeable and being a good fit for the school–community. Be pleasant, smile, and try to resonate with the cultural norms and values of the board.

## Transition to Central Office

If you work in Central Office, the most significant difference is that you are no longer in regular contact with students. As a Central Office leader, you will experience a significant shift, a redefinition, in how you fulfill your vision on a system-wide basis. The advantage that a principal has in moving to Central Office is his or her ability to relate to school principals. Use your valuable experience and help coach them and teach them through their problems. That is one example of what I mean by redefining your practice—a shift from coaching teachers and students to coaching principals.

Another critical shift is that you lose your constituencies. As a principal, parents, students, and teachers are your constituents, and you are the leader of the school. In Central Office, you have one constituent—the superintendent. You must put your ego aside and serve your superintendent and his or her team. Your voice and visibility are limited.

Another big change is the challenge in balancing the "paperwork" with contact with the schools. Every Central Office person makes a commitment to "get into the school buildings," but then the reality of grants, budgets, and new regulations you are in charge of rise up and engulf you. Unless you get into the schools, you lose touch. The challenge of maintaining contact falls hardest on special education administrators because of all their regulations-based responsibilities. The challenge is also great for assistant superintendents for instruction, with the numerous state accountability reports that you must provide for the variety of state grants that the district receives.

## Congratulations, You Got the Job, Now What?

After going through an exhausting job search process, finally you have been appointed to your new leadership position and are starting the job. Of course, you want to be successful. Although you would never admit it, you are feeling insecure. You haven't formed trusting relationships as yet, you're not fully familiar with all of the aspects of your new responsibilities, you are trying to figure out the culture of the school–community, you don't want to overstep your authority and offend anyone, and perhaps most importantly, you don't know the internal politics. Most of your peers seem to be welcoming, and your staff appears to be friendly, but they are cautious and a bit uncomfortable around you. Of course, you want to make a good initial impression, but you need to figure out the social, political, and professional norms and expectations.

The best advice is to be cautious, go slow and steady, ask questions, be friendly, and pick "low lying fruit," that is, easily accomplished goals which can be quickly achieved. However, you recognize that you are the "new kid in the class" and feel as if all eyes are on you, that you are being judged, and talked about. Most of your colleagues have been friendly and offered their assistance. Still, be careful about forming alliances and with whom you confide. Remember that your priority is to please your direct supervisor(s) and gain his/her confidence.

The trickiest job is figuring out the politics, that is who is allied with whom. On the surface it probably looks like one happy family. As you develop a clearer picture, you may find there may be bad histories among the cast of characters. There may be power conflicts, favoritism, grudges, and jealousies among and between colleagues—some of which are clear, however, much of which is under the radar. Therefore, you must be alert to behaviors and subtle signs that form a pattern as to the nature of the internal politics, and then you must figure out how to negotiate and navigate the politics.

### *Twelve Tips for New Leaders to be Successful*

What should you do to maximize your success in your new position? You have been a successful teacher who enjoyed a reputation of being friendly, supportive, and collegial. Now, in a new leadership role, you are expected to deal effectively with new and/or perhaps old colleagues who may be resistant to your leadership; parents who are dissatisfied with how their child had been treated in the past, and more senior administrators who assign you demanding responsibilities (student discipline, supervising resistant faculty members, revising a curriculum, lunchroom and bus supervision, parent complaints, etc.).

You may be a new principal who had successfully served as an assistant principal. As an assistant principal, you essentially had only one constituent to satisfy, and that was your principal. Now, you are faced with satisfying multiple constituencies, which include the faculty, the student body, parent groups

(PTA, athletic booster, music boosters, and special education parents), Central Office administrators, and various unions.

The failure of administrators is often rooted in the inability to (1) establish trusting relationships, (2) solve problems by developing and implementing workable solutions, (3) get the staff's "buy in" to your decision-making process and leadership style, and (4) earn respect. Here are my suggestions as to how you can be a successful new leader:

1. Conduct one-on-one, get-acquainted meetings with all faculty members and leaders of each constituent group. Ask, "What in your opinion are the greatest strengths and greatest needs of the school?"
2. Make yourself visible and accessible to all members of the school–community. This means get out of your office and into the classrooms and corridors and interact with attendees at school events.
3. Demonstrate that you respect the school culture and the past practices of those who have preceded you.
4. Seek out honest feedback and advice from staff. Listen, assess, and act based on relevant feedback.
5. Communicate realistic and fair expectations with clarity; provide opportunities for input and discussion.
6. Recruit effective staff members whenever possible who will strengthen your team. This includes secretaries, custodians, and aides.
7. Keep your personal, political, and religious views to yourself.
8. Limit socializing with the staff after school. Alcohol tends to loosen inhibitions and can lead to inappropriate behavior and speech. Alcohol and leaderships do not mix.
9. Avoid offering your opinions or taking sides in matters of district and/or school politics.
10. Do due diligence regarding important problems that you encounter by walking around them 360 degrees and examining the issues and their implications from every perspective before deciding.
11. Don't be reluctant to ask for help or seek advice.
12. Keep a reflective journal in order to process and reflect upon your thoughts and actions.

## A New Job: An Opportunity for Reinvention

Starting a new job is an opportunity to reinvent yourself. It can be a chance to leave whatever baggage you might have had behind you and get a fresh start.

Aside from doing the obvious things like making a good first impression by introducing yourself to the various stakeholder groups, coming up to speed on what is going on, and doing a "listening tour," which all are certainly good things to do, you need to consider the following:

- **Be humble**—don't brag about what you've done. Give credit to your team members. They will appreciate the recognition and in return speak well of you. No one likes a braggart.

- **Never overpromise or under-deliver**—do not make promises that you might not be able to achieve. When you set a goal, make it measurable so that there is a standard that's modest enough so that it will be readily achieved. It's always better to exceed the standard so it's perceived that you overachieved.

- **Do not criticize your predecessor**—whoever your predecessor might have been or done, or whatever you've heard about him or her, be aware that he or she also had admirers who would resent hearing that you are critical and will hold it against you.

- **Don't pick unnecessary fights**—your early cheerleaders' support is newborn and therefore tentative. It takes time to achieve solid support that you can depend upon should you run into a problem. If you do encounter a potentially divisive issue, then find middle ground and attempt a compromise. You can't afford to go to war without strong allies.

- **Seek out advisors and mentors**—most influencers are flattered when asked for their input. They feel respected, validated, and appreciated. This is an effective way of building supportive constituencies.

- **Build loyal relationships with your supervisors**—effective leaders need to rely upon the loyalty of their direct reports. Leaking confidential information, criticizing and undermining decisions, and personality assassinations are all examples of destructive actions that leaders can suffer from disloyal subordinates. Your bosses need your loyalty. Demonstrate your loyalty by never publicly contradicting them, speaking positively about them, and acting in concert with their priorities. Hopefully they will in return be loyal to you; however, too often loyalty tends to be a one-way street.

## Politics and Power of School Leadership

We all know that local education is fueled by politics and the use of power; however, we seldom talk about it publicly. To understand the dynamics of politics and power is to be empowered. The principles that go to the heart of these dynamics are: (1) the more power is exercised, the weaker it becomes; (2) the most potent form of power is perceived power; (3) the most outspoken critics of school leaders are imposters; and (4) the real power resides with the kids and their parents. Let's analyze these dynamics.

**More Is Less**—Mr. Smith, sixth grade teacher, threatens his students that if they continue to misbehave, he will send them to the office. Johnny steps over the line and is sent to the office. A lesson in power, right? Well, not so fast. Thirty minutes later, Johnny returns with a subtle smirk on his face. Then Mary acts out, and she's sent to the office. She returns in 20 minutes. Okay Mr. Smith, what is happening to your authority? Lessons learned, don't make threats that you can't uphold; and the more you exercise your power, the more it will be tested, and the faster it will be eroded. The outcome is that you'll only be shooting blanks.

**Perceived Power**—if you are perceived to hold power, then you have power. If your constituents believe you can make changes, you can get things done, you can influence other powerful players, then that perception of your influence gives you power. Proportionately, the greater and more widespread the perception, the greater the power is. But, be careful. If you exercise that power, and you're ineffective, then that power dissipates and erodes exponentially. Therefore, use your influence prudently—don't overreach.

**Imposters**—An angry parent calls you regarding a routine and justifiable policy change you have just made. After failing to convince the caller of the reasonableness of your action, the parent threatens to call your supervisor, get the PTA involved, and call all of his friends and storm the next Board of Education meeting, if you don't immediately rescind the policy. It sounds like you're really drawing fire from a powerful person. Remember, you can't reason with an unreasonable person. But you can disagree. Now, I'm not an advocate of poking someone in the eye, hanging up the phone, or telling him where to go. Never go out of your way to make a situation worse by being rude, raising your voice, or being obnoxious because then you'll be accused of unprofessional behavior and that will become the issue. However, don't capitulate to a bully. Most decent people have been bullied, know bullies when they see one, and don't like bullies. My advice is to say: "Well, I see we're in disagreement. Of course, it's your prerogative to do what you please. Would you like the phone number of my supervisor?" Offering a phone number will signal that you're not intimidated. Then get a quick message to your supervisor and the president of the PTA to explain why they may be getting a call. Remember, whoever gets the message out first usually is in a stronger position. Let the bully do his thing. He's an imposter.

**The Real Power**—about forty years ago, a veteran principal gave me one of the best pieces of advice I ever got. He said: "Go to work every day and bring your A game. Take good care of the kids. If the kids like you, they'll go home and tell their parents how wonderful you are, and then the parents will like you. If the kids and the parents like you, and you don't do something really dumb, then nobody can harm you." A word from the wise!

## *The Need for New Leadership: Final Thoughts*

What can be said of the state of public education in the twenty-first century? With shrinking budgets, changing demographics, renewed and revamped accountability measures, the polarization of politics, and the banning of books, our worst times can be the best of times for the most capable, talented, and committed educators to rise to the challenges and make an impact in our field and on our society. There is a need for high-quality, creative, inspired new leadership if we are to fulfill our social contract with children and families.

The United States is slowly emerging from the pandemic and seems to be heading into a recession. For some leaders, the convergence of these significant issues has caused an atmosphere of panic because we will have to do more with less, while for others it is an opportunity to rethink the possibilities of public education.

The changing demographics of the United States and the ensuing changes in the student population in public schools will provide the impetus for school leaders to pay more attention to being culturally responsive, providing equity in the manner in which we provide opportunities, differentiating instruction, and nurturing meaningful relationships with students who may be perceived as "different." Ethnic minorities, now 37 percent of the U.S. population, are projected to comprise 57 percent of the population by the year 2060. The total minority population will more than double, from 116.2 million to 241.3 million, over this period. Inherent in the changing demographics are also projected increases in students who are learning English as a new language and students of color. Clearly, the pedagogy must be in tune with the vast changes of our landscape.

As a school leader, you are held accountable for raising student achievement. Your job and those of your teachers determine the future competence of our workforce and our economic future. As an educational leader you must be prepared and committed to make a difference. You must articulate and fulfill that commitment. Here are a few ideas you should consider about raising student achievement:

a. Historically, you are not the first and only school leader to be asked to reinvent American education.
b. American education was reinvented several times; during the depression, post–World War II, and after Sputnik.
c. You are best served when you are supported by a team that shares similar guiding principles and vision.
d. There are promising research-based approaches and documented case studies of leaders who have successfully turned schools and districts around.

As a candidate, you must communicate your passion, knowledge, commitment, and vision to becoming a transitional leader in these challenging times. I wish you the best as you embark on the next step in your career journey into school leadership. The field of education needs YOU to lead us during this challenging era. I suggest that, if you follow my strategies, then you will eventually hear those magic words: "YOU'RE HIRED!"

# ABOUT THE AUTHOR

Larry Aronstein, Ed.D.

**Dr. Larry Aronstein** has spent 50 years in public education, having started as a science teacher in New York City, then working as a principal at the elementary, middle school, and high school levels, and assistant superintendent for curriculum and instruction, retiring as Superintendent of Schools, and then serving as an Interim Superintendent on Long Island. He consults and trains school leaders and aspiring leaders in how to get their leadership jobs. Many credit Dr. Aronstein with leading the Glen Cove and Copiague school districts into periods of renaissance. He most recently served as the Interim Superintendent of the North Babylon Schools on Long Island. He relishes the challenge of coaching supervisors and teachers to excel as instructional leaders. Long before moving to Long Island, Dr. Aronstein was lauded for his superior leadership skills, winning the Massachusetts Principal of the Year award. In addition, during his tenure at the John Glenn Middle School in Bedford, Massachusetts, he was invited to the White House where the school was awarded the prestigious National Recognition Award. Dr. Aronstein has published dozens of articles in leading educational periodicals, including *Educational Leadership*, *NASSP Bulletin*, *Science Teacher*, and *Action Learning*, an ASCD publication. He has also consulted in dozens of districts throughout the United States and Germany. In addition, he was the founder and director of the highly respected Long Island Leadership Academy, mentoring scores of educational leaders.

CPSIA information can be obtained
at www.ICGtesting.com
Printed in the USA
JSHW082137310523
42528JS00001B/3